To Emma, my inspiration.

*To all those yet to start their journey to recovery,
and the ones who never had the chance.*

Contents

Acknowledgments

My heartfelt thanks to Gill Tavner for taking time out to support me editorially and also to Alison Hull and all the team at Lion Hudson. Your wisdom and patience have been inspiring. With special thanks to my mother for believing in me and encouraging me to to write.

Prologue

My right leg was jiggling. I pushed firmly on my knee with a sweaty palm, hoping one of the cameras hadn't already picked up on the involuntary movement. I counted at least ten cameras in the brightly lit studio. Some were fixed to the floor, too big to move; other, hand-held models zipped around like insects, while the mid-sized versions seemed to hover just above the floor. One was even mounted on a long arm, controlled remotely by someone I couldn't see.

"Five minutes to broadcast – and remember, don't pick your nose, and if you do fall asleep, do it with your eyes open. Above all, never, never look at the cameras." The studio manager sounded like an old pro; he knew how to make the audience laugh. There was nothing he hadn't seen before, nothing was going to faze him.

Actually, where was I supposed to look? I wiped away a bead of sweat before it trickled down my powdered face.

The last empty seat had just been filled a few rows behind me and now there was a buzz of expectation as the studio guests pointed out the celebrities to their neighbours. I fidgeted on my front-row seat, trying in vain to get comfortable. The little studio was now packed. The lady on my right, elegant in a short red polka-dot dress, seemed familiar to me. I tried, but couldn't place her. I knew the comedian on my left though; he had flown out to Bosnia to entertain the soldiers when I was still in the Army. That was fifteen years ago. He'd gone public about his addiction to drugs and alcohol since then and was the star of a recent celebrity reality show.

"OK, everyone, welcome to the *Great Live Debt Debate*. We're two minutes to go." It was Nick Farrari, the TV presenter and our host for the show that was about to be broadcast live to millions of people.

"Tonight is all about you. The success of this programme is down to how involved you want to be. Out front here we'll have the panel. If you don't agree with anything they or anyone else says, shout out. No point putting your hand up politely like you did at school; you'll be there all night. Just shout. We're after the 10 p.m. watershed, so we don't mind if your language is colourful, but see those guys over there?" He pointed towards two body builders lurking in the shadows at the back of the room. "That's security. If you're disruptive, you'll be taken out. Now, let's practise some applause."

It took us three attempts before Nick was happy.

"OK, sixty seconds. And these chairs," he said, pointing his clipboard at the front of the stage, "will be occupied by members of the panel. We'll change the folk up here at each interval, depending on how the debate is going. Remember, challenge them, don't give them an easy ride. Some of you have come a long way; this is your chance to be on TV. Let's make some noise!"

I'd made a terrible mistake. I didn't belong here. I wanted to walk out, but I was trapped. I knew if I stood up, I'd feel the hands of security pushing me back down in my seat. I made up my mind not to say anything. I wasn't about to shout anything out.

"OK, Justyn, we need to wire you up." It was the floor manager and, as he clipped the radio mic to my shirt, I knew it wouldn't be possible to hide.

The debate kicked off and after two minutes, I was horrified. People were ranting and raving, fingers were being pointed and accusations flew. Here were debtors who blamed the banks for giving them credit, bankers blaming the debtors for being irresponsible. The room was blue with language I hadn't heard since leaving the Army. There were people on benefits facing a life of poverty, and celebrities who had gone bankrupt rather than pay their tax bill. On the big screen shocking stories of debt and misery were shown, stoking up the fires of disagreement and fuelling yet more arguments. I slid down even further in my uncomfortable chair. I didn't belong there; I wished I'd never agreed to it. It was a freak show and I was one of the freaks, about to be publicly humiliated in front of the nation.

Time passed and I began to hope I'd been forgotten. I cringed as the celebrities either side of me vociferously took different sides of the debate, shouting each other down, one in my right ear, the other in my left. Meanwhile the remote camera hovered close by, like a cobra about to strike. As the final commercial break signified the end of the third quarter, I was convinced I'd been forgotten.

What did I have to add to the debate anyway? Yes, I'd got myself into debt, but it was my own fault, to feed an addiction. I hadn't taken out loans because I'd lost my job. I took them out before I lost my job. I hadn't got into debt because I fell ill, although addiction, at its worst, can be as debilitating as any sickness. They would never call on me to sit up on the stage in one of the four chairs. These had been occupied by an ex-England footballer fallen on tough times, an MP, a famous Olympian and other well-known faces, all with their eloquent opinions and confident delivery.

"And we need Justyn, please." I looked around; maybe there was another Justyn. But the floor manager was looking at me. This was not good.

The makeup lady fussed around me, dabbing my face with a brush that made me want to sneeze. I felt the heat of the studio lights, so much brighter on the stage. I felt pinned down as the muscles in my chest contracted, my throat dried and my stomach tied itself in granny knots. I looked at all the faces in the audience. Red light – we were on air again.

The screen at the back of the studio came to life and this time it was my story being broadcast live to the nation. After three days of filming me at my home, the programme makers had crammed my story into a two-minute clip. They chose to show a sequence when I had broken down and cried during the filming, as I recalled the awful depths of my gambling addiction – how my wife had left me, taking my two little boys with her to the safety of her parents' house while my life imploded in an almost terminal act of self-destruction.

As the studio lights came up, I was choked up once more. I could hardly speak and there were tears in my eyes. For the first time that evening a hush descended on the studio audience. No one was finger pointing or shouting out. I saw genuine compassion in most of the faces looking back at me.

"So, Justyn, you're the victim here," said the floor manager. "You've served in the Army, seen operational service, but I can see you're broken. What would you say to the banks? What help did they give you to help you get out of debt? Do you blame them for getting into so much debt in the first place?"

"No, I don't blame the banks," I replied. "I have no one to blame but myself. I take 100 per cent responsibility."

If I said much more than that, I don't remember the words. But I do remember the relief I felt at the sound of spontaneous applause.

On Saturday, 17 August 2013 approximately 5 million people read a double-page article in the *Daily Mail*, which featured the confession of a man with everything to lose, who had lost everything. My motivation for going public was very simple. I wanted people to be more aware of the devastatingly destructive impact gambling has on some people's lives. Almost three quarters of all adults in the UK, male and female, have gambled at some point over the last twelve months. We are constantly bombarded by TV advertisements, intrusive invitations in our social media timelines and sponsorship targeted to have the maximum impact on the young.

The vast majority of people gamble responsibly, but there are probably half a million people in misery in the UK because they can't stop gambling. And for every problem gambler there are people around them suffering the consequences of the problem gambler's actions: broken homes, damaged friendships, work colleagues who have to pick up the pieces. Some problem gamblers face jail sentences; others even commit suicide.

Compulsive gambling is one of the least understood addictions; in fact it has only been recognized as such quite recently. There is a perception that gambling is a lifestyle choice. I would argue that for some it was once a choice, but is now a miserable sentence, where the inmate sees no way out.

When I placed my first bet, I was a man who had everything: home, wife, children, job, security and self-respect. I had everything to lose. What compelled me to risk it all, for no certain return? Do some of us possess a gene that predisposes us to addictive behaviour, or perhaps a specific character trait, like the fatal flaw of a tragic hero? Or is it entirely due to circumstances – outside forces beyond our control and sometimes beyond our comprehension? Or is it both? Or neither? I don't know the answer.

Whatever the cause, the consequences are fearful. In sharing my terrible story, I have come to understand I was by no means the first to throw my life away. But I would like to be one of the last.

Many people close to me were angry that I shared my private story so publicly that day in August 2013. It was not an easy thing to do, but I now know that the article in the national press helped many people to recognize truths about their own lives and to see that there is hope.

When I realized that I wasn't going to be ostracized, I felt relief. That's how I felt the evening I walked out of the TV studio. Compulsive gambling, like many addictions, can be a lonely place. I want people to know that they are not alone; that they won't be judged if they talk about their habit that's become a compulsion; that there is hope, a way out. There is light at the end of the tunnel.

Tonbridge
18 March 2014

PART 1

Beginnings

To *understand the future, we need to understand the past.*
WINSTON CHURCHILL

CHAPTER 1

Early Introduction

I was seven years old and I was so excited. It was my turn to spend the weekend at Granny and Grandpa's house. With two brothers and three sisters, exclusive time with parents or grandparents was rare.

At home, with so many mouths to feed, food was often in short supply. Every meal was a race to finish first just in case there were any seconds. In contrast, a visit to Grandma's was a gastronomic treat. My grandmother always cooked enough for an army, especially puddings. At every lunchtime and suppertime, she produced plate after plate of "sweets", as she called them. Lemon tarts, pavlovas, chocolate gateaux, ice cream, tinned mandarins and always a freshly made egg custard, sprinkled with cinnamon. My grandmother was as generous with her self as with her food. A very warm person, she loved to cuddle us. She played card games of "Snap" and "Pairs" with infinite patience.

While my grandmother liked to spoil us with her glorious food, my grandfather's way of showing love to his grandchildren might be a trip to a football match, or sometimes to the toyshop, where I almost invariably chose a model aeroplane. My grandfather was a bank manager before he retired, but during the war he had served in the Royal Air Force. Although he never once spoke to me about the war, I felt his approval whenever I chose a model RAF aircraft. It wasn't until he died that I discovered he had served in RAF Intelligence and was responsible for planning the mission to deliver

Douglas Bader's replacement prosthetic leg to the French Resistance in 1942, after the one-legged fighter ace had been shot down.

Today's visit to my grandparents was one of the more special ones: Grandpa and I were going to see a live football match. I was mad about football. Each week, while my sisters carefully put their pocket money in their piggy banks, I took mine straight to the village newsagent and spent every penny I had on *Shoot* magazine. I knew all the players and the League positions of every team in the first three divisions. At seven, I still believed I would one day play centre forward for my beloved Tottenham Hotspur. In the playground at school, I was always Glen Hoddle.

As a news reporter for the local paper, my Uncle Graham would occasionally be sent to cover the Tonbridge Angels. Today they were playing Broadstairs, and we were to be in the press box. Living with my grandmother's cooking meant that Grandpa was a large man. Sometimes, although we had been allocated seats in the press box, there would be no room for me to sit, but I didn't mind standing. At half time Grandpa always gave me a pound note. Clutching it, I would follow the crowds towards the bar where I always bought a bottle of coke and a packet of Golden Wonder crisps. A green bag if they had any left, blue if not. Such small things were a real treat.

The match today was an away fixture. I could hardly contain my excitement as we sped in Uncle Graham's old Fiat 125 along the A20. The car was shuddering as it reached its top performance (probably no more than 50 mph), the thrilling sensation perfectly matching my mood. We arrived early for the game and parked near the stadium, leaving time to walk into the town centre, only a few minutes away. There, I found a huge toy shop: the biggest one I had ever seen.

Although Grandpa had already bought me a model plane that morning, and although I knew how careful he was with money, I persuaded him to take me inside. Reluctantly, he followed me in. The shop was an Aladdin's cave, packed full of the most wonderful toys, games and models. I can still remember how the shelves towered above me, crammed with toys I could only dream of owning. I think I must have asked for something, because I will never forget what my grandfather said next: they were words that may have had a profound effect on me more than thirty years later. As I had expected, he told me very firmly that the answer was no. But he must have seen the hurt in my face, because he then said that if he won the pools that day he would buy me everything in the shop.

I couldn't believe what I was hearing. The thought of owning toys that my friends would envy was almost too much to take in. I took him round every shelf, pointing out the toys I wanted. I didn't want to leave that shop. Although I had all the fun things in life, like brothers and sisters and a huge garden to make camps and play in, I didn't have the material things my school friends had.

In the end, Uncle Graham came in and managed to persuade me that if we didn't leave, we would miss the game. On the way back to the stadium, I asked Grandpa what the pools were.

"I guess the scores in every football match in the top leagues. If I get enough right, I'll win lots of money." Draws were what he wanted and draws where both sides scored, called score-draws, were the best.

Having worked in a bank for most of his adult life, my grandfather was brilliant with figures. One day he took me to a fund-raising fete in a church hall. There was a huge jar of sweets on one of the wooden trestles. For 10p you could guess the number of sweets – the guess closest to the correct number would win the whole jar. Grandpa picked up the jar and studied it for a minute before confidently saying a number. We went home with the sweets. His "guess" had been out by only two! From that day on he was a legend to me, and I think I told him so because, very humbly, he told me it was nothing really. He had just counted the depth and width of sweets and applied a cylindrical volume calculation. That just made me worship him all the more.

As we took our places high up in the stand I just knew Grandpa was going to win the pools. I don't remember anything about the game. I spent the whole time picturing my friends' faces when I turned up at school with my shiny new *Starsky and Hutch* car (large-scale, red with the white stripes down the side).

I began to feel slight concern when we drove out of the town. I had assumed that Grandpa would know the pools result before we left for home. I'd been dreaming of returning to the toyshop that day, before it closed.

"I won't know until all the results are in," he told me. I didn't hide my disappointment. In a family of six children, you very quickly learn how to pull on an adult's emotional strings.

"Don't worry, Justo. I'll take you back there if we win. I promise." He had said "if *we* win"; I felt included and excited to be part of the game.

We got back to my grandparents' house just as the final scores were being announced. The adults sat in armchairs near the TV set, marking off the scores on cards. I found a place on the floor near Grandpa's feet. I still had no doubts that he would win, but as time passed there was no confirmation from him. The Final Score Announcer finally closed with the words, "And the Pools forecast is… low." I had no idea what that meant and I kept looking up at him expectantly. Eventually he became quite cross with me as he puffed away on his pipe, so I hid my impatience.

I didn't give up hope for several days and still fell asleep each night for a week imagining what I would do with all the toys. I felt a sense of loss when I realized Grandpa had not won. Some of his legendary powers wore off in my mind and I think I was cross with him. He probably felt he'd let me down in some way and we never spoke about it again. It was my first taste of gambling and, although I find it hard to believe that it could have contributed to my downfall years later, the fact that this event sticks in my mind so clearly suggests it might have been significant in some way.

Early Introduction

In contrast to my loving paternal grandmother, Grandpa was a difficult man to please. I don't ever remember hugging him and I was always a little wary of upsetting him, but I so wanted to please him, to feel his love and approval. The only time I ever kissed him was on the day he died, several years after that day we went to watch the football. Dad must have had a call from the hospital, because I remember he bundled us all into the car and off we went. Grandpa was asleep and looked thinner than I had ever seen him before. I said goodbye and kissed his cheek. I remember very clearly that I dropped a tear on his face and felt scared that it might wake him and then he would be cross. But he was still asleep when I turned round at the door of the ward to wave a last goodbye.

Chapter 2

Early Loss

I never knew my maternal grandfather, Tom Rees. He died suddenly in a hotel room in New York at the age of fifty-eight. I was a year old. Although I have no memory of him, as I grew up I sensed his loss in those around me, particularly in my grandmother, Jean, whom we all called Otty.

"The Boss", as he was known, even to his own children, was, by all accounts, a huge character. I still meet people who remember him. I never miss the opportunity to ask them what he was like, or if they recall any particular adventure they can share with me about my famous grandfather who was a friend of the Duke and Duchess of Windsor, mentor to the American evangelist Billy Graham, and a man who had filled the Royal Albert Hall more than fifty times with people who came to hear him speak.

People say he was a terrific orator, brilliant when speaking to thousands of people. But they also say he was wonderful one to one; attentive, wise and funny. Although I can watch films several times, I don't usually like to read a book twice, but I don't know how many times I have read my grandfather's biography. Otty wrote it a few years after he died. I particularly loved the bits about my family history, from which I learned about several generations of our colourful predecessors. I read it for the first time when I was ten years old. I wanted to know more, so Mum and I went for a long walk along a cliff path in Devon and she answered all my questions, adding detail to the beautiful picture in my mind that is my family tree, my heritage and my roots.

Both my maternal grandparents were born into relatively privileged families, although, over the years, the fortunes had dwindled. The Boss's grandfather invented a clasp fastener that's still used today on ladies' under-garments! Otty's grandfather made a fortune in tobacco during the First World War and owned an estate in Scotland as well as a huge property in Bishops Avenue, Highgate, where my mother was born.

When The Boss died we all moved into an old farm house. It was big enough to divide into three. On one side lived Otty, and the other side we converted into a flat for my great-grandmother, The Boss's mother. My parents and I lived in the middle with my elder sister Sarah, until I was five years old. We left that house abruptly after just two years, and it wasn't until I was in my early teens that my mother decided she could tell me about the sinister things that she, and others in my family, experienced during the brief time we lived there. My sister often talked about the "grey people who lived upstairs". Even I can remember a terrible rotting smell that used to pervade one of the rooms at certain times of day. It wasn't the drains.

Otty had a live-in secretary when we first moved in. On the second night her secretary felt herself being pulled out of bed by her legs. When it happened again the next night, she left and never came back. Window frames would blow out unexpectedly and the same picture fell from the wall time after time. It came to a head one night when Otty was asleep. She woke to the sound of heavy footsteps ascending the stairs to her bedroom. The experience was enough to put her in a psychiatric hospital for three months. I remember that absence.

The local vicar was invited to do an exorcism, but after researching the property, he called for a bishop! One day Mum bumped into the previous owner, who asked her how the family were settling in. When she told him about these strange events, he said he'd been worried that might happen. When he had experienced similar events, he decided to do some research. He discovered that a previous owner, at the turn of the last century, was rumoured to have been a Satanist. There were other local stories about this colourful figure. Since then, one person from every family who had lived in Otty's side of the house had suffered depression or ill health.

My parents quickly sold the house, but Mum insisted on telling the new owners that she thought it might be haunted. They were delighted and told my parents they were spiritualists. My mother discovered some years later that the couple had split up and the husband, who stayed on alone at the property, committed suicide in the garage.

We moved to a suburban estate in Tunbridge Wells. In contrast to the farmhouse, our new home had very little to offer a young boy who loved to explore.

I was very close to Otty; we had a special relationship. As her first grandson, I think I was probably treated indulgently. I once overheard my father telling my mother I was "being spoilt". I used to sneak round to Otty's rooms. Whatever she was doing, she always had time for me. I loved listening to her stories. She made characters from the Bible come to life; to this day they seem real to me. Although I realize now that she was in the grip of a great depression, she introduced me to some of the things I still love to this day.

Otty was a writer, an artist and she loved playing golf. I often caddied for her. She had so much patience with me; as a six-year-old, I was hardly strong enough to lift her golf bag, let alone tell the difference between a driver and a wedge, but still she took me to the golf club where she was Ladies' Captain and paid me one pound per round. She arranged golf lessons for me and she introduced me to restaurants.

The best treats were visits to the department store in Tunbridge Wells where she had an account. The staff in the toy department all knew her by name. We would take the lift to the top-floor restaurant where I ordered the same thing every time – a "Womble" Burger with chips and beans, and tomato ketchup served on the side in a stainless-steel egg cup. This was followed by a Knickerbocker Glory, brought to the table by a smartly dressed waitress.

I thought Otty was the best grandmother in the world. She didn't shower us with sweets; she just made us all laugh, told exciting stories and let us use her bed as a trampoline! I still treasure the box of oil paints she bought me when I was seven. She didn't just buy me some paints, though; she gave me lessons in how to use them. Those paints were one of the precious things I would later salvage from the wreck I made of my life. Otty and I remained very close, right up until the day she died.

When I was ten years old Otty suffered a stroke, so we converted our lounge to a bedroom for her. Every day before I left for school I used to go in and talk to her. The conversations were rather one-sided, as she hadn't spoken much since the stroke. I held her hand as she lay in her bed, and told her she would be with The Boss in heaven soon. It must have been painful for her and her words were jumbled, but she spoke to me and smiled a lopsided smile. I think she was trying to say, "I'm ready, I can't wait, I'm going home." They were the last words she ever spoke. She died later that day. She had lived for ten years after The Boss died, but her broken heart never really recovered from the loss of her soulmate.

Otty's death had a profound effect on me. I was heartbroken and lost for a while without her, but it strengthened a growing faith in me. I was given her precious Bible and I read it cover to cover before my eleventh birthday. It was full of little notes and her favourite verses were all underlined.

Before her death, I had been almost uncontrollable at school and always in trouble. I often took a humiliating beating from the teacher in front of the class. I still remember the intensity of the pain across the backs of my bare legs. Summer, winter, rain or shine, I was the only boy who wore shorts every day until I left junior school. It seems that even these beatings didn't stop me, and visits to the headmaster's office for further discipline were frequent. I don't think anyone knew how to tame me. Today, I would have been diagnosed with some hyperactive disorder, but in those days I was just labelled as naughty. I am certain I deserved every beating I received. I was, without doubt, the naughtiest child in the school.

For months after Otty died I imagined her watching me from heaven. I was desperate to please her still. I had felt loved by her and this love had caused me to respect her and always be on my best behaviour around her. Now she was in heaven, I didn't want her to see me getting into trouble at school. This was just what I needed. Everyone noticed the change in my behaviour after her death. I grew up and started to take my schooling more seriously. I discovered school was much more fun when it didn't involve being smacked. Even my class teacher, a wonderful old lady called Miss Crutch, commented on the change in me and asked me what had happened. I told her I had changed because I was a Christian and was trying to follow what the Bible told me to do. She must have been impressed because she asked me which part of the Bible she should read first.

It was around that time that I joined a swimming club in the nearby town and discovered a talent that would channel my energy for the next eight years and give me a focus that would take me round the world in competitive events.

CHAPTER 3

Early Idyll

Born on 14 February 1969, I was a very, very ugly baby with a squished face and spiky dark hair. One morning, when I was out in the pushchair, a friend of my mum took one look at me and said in horror, "Oh, what a lovely... bonnet!"

I am the eldest son among six children. My one elder sister, Sarah, was born just over a year before me. I have two younger brothers, Duncan and Richard, and two younger sisters, Naomie and Sarah Jane, or SJ. My parents adopted SJ when she was seven. They had known her mother and father. When her mother died suddenly they promised her father that they would look after SJ if anything happened to him. Sadly, very soon afterwards her father died quite suddenly of a heart attack. SJ is a brilliant sister and very much one of "The Clan". My early childhood seemed to be like one endless happy summer of picnics in bluebell-draped woods, building dams in streams, swimming in lakes, holidays in Devon and laughter-filled games with my five brothers and sisters.

We all have heroes, people we look up to and respect. Without any doubt, my greatest hero is my mum, Jen. She is more than seventy years old and in constant pain from rheumatoid arthritis, but she travels the length and breadth of the country, leaving in the early hours and driving up and down motorways, to talk to groups of people, mostly women, bringing hope to those who hurt in some way, often through broken relationships, but also through bereavement and loss. Despite great setbacks in her own life, her complete lack of selfishness draws people to her and gives them hope when everything around them seems hopeless and bleak. I have seen it happen time and time again. She keeps an open house and I see broken people, often tearful, walk through her front door, only to leave an hour later with a smile on their faces. When my whole world fell apart, Mum gave me hope in my darkest hour. She didn't judge me, didn't feel sorry for me. She didn't even try to advise me. I just felt her love, unconditional and genuine.

She met my dad, Tony, in the sixties. They were childhood sweethearts. As teenagers, they both sang in my Uncle Justyn's band, which enjoyed minor success with a record deal, a TV appearance and airtime on radio. Although they clashed when they first met, they were married within two years. The Boss, who had great aspirations for my mother, didn't really approve of my dad at first. Although very dashing and handsome, Dad was a schoolteacher from a lower-middle-class family. In contrast to the affluent heritage of my mum's side of the family, the Larcombe family tree can only be traced back to my great-grandfather who, as an abandoned infant, was found and taken in by two spinster sisters in a small village in Somerset. They named the young boy after the small valley where he was found.

However, The Boss could not for long deny the obvious love between his daughter and Tony Larcombe. He eventually gave his blessing and bought them a house as a wedding present. They had over a thousand guests at their wedding reception, which was held at Hildenborough Hall, a huge stately home that The Boss and Otty had opened as a Christian conference centre. The rambling mock-Tudor building was set high on the Kent Downs near Sevenoaks. As a boy I spent long summers there. It's the headquarters of a successful holiday company now.

The house was built in the 1930s for Sir Oliver Lyle, the sugar magnate. At the front of the house are terraces with stunning views across the Weald of Kent and Sussex. On one of the terraces is the swimming pool where I almost drowned at the age of six. The pool was kidney shaped and had a very steep slope between the shallow end and the deep end. I hadn't learned to swim and I can clearly remember playing alone in the shallow end. Before I knew it my feet were slipping down the slope and my head went under. I looked up and all I could see was clear blue sky and a very bright sun. I don't know how long I was under, but there was no way back up that slope. I was heading to the bottom when I saw the outline of a face in silhouette. It seemed to block out the sun, while being framed by its rays. A hand reached down to me and I grabbed it. My angel was a lady called Sue who must have seen me disappear beneath the surface. I bump into her quite regularly now and still thank her each time for saving my life.

Drowning was just one of the many dangerous things I tried. At nursery I fell off the slide head-first and concussed myself; I drove my bike through a glass window and, on another occasion, down a manhole so deep that I couldn't get out. The skin on my knees and elbows never lasted very long. I was showing early signs of thrill-seeking, perhaps even recklessness.

As well as the swimming pool, the Hall also had croquet lawns, three tennis courts, an indoor shooting range, a clay-pigeon trap, a go-cart track, a little golf course, a secret passage, stables and even its own chapel. It was a wonderful place for a small boy to play. Best of all, during the long summer weeks, the guests that came to stay were all families, so it was filled with other children for me to play with. The only sadness was that they always left after a week and I had to make friends all over again.

A portrait of The Boss hung in the panelled library of the Hall. As a child this picture fascinated me and I often snuck off to the library to gaze up at the picture hanging above the fireplace. The portrait was painted in such a way that my grandfather's eyes seemed to follow me around the huge room. It somehow brought him to life for me.

I loved my visits to the Hall because there was so much to explore. I didn't enjoy living on a housing estate in a town. I loved the wide-open space of the countryside. So I was pleased when I was told we were moving back to the country.

One day in 1976, towards the end of one of the hottest summers on record, Dad drove the family car along a country lane. The grass in the fields on both sides of the road looked dry and yellow, scorched by the intense sun. He stopped the car at the end of a long driveway and we jumped out, impatient to see our new home.

"This is the house," Dad said. I wasn't looking at the house; all I could see were the climbing trees and a huge garden to run around in. It was an idyllic place for a young boy. I had freedom to roam and walked the two miles every day to the little village primary school, or at weekends to the sweet shop to spend my pocket money on football magazines. Most days we had friends round for tea, as well as the two children Mum child-minded. I just don't know how we all fitted around the dining-room table.

The girls had ballet classes on Mondays and I went to Cubs in the village hall. To get from one place to another we all had to pack into a white camper van called the "Chugger". That was the noise it made as it struggled up the hills, full to overflowing with kids of all sizes. It broke down on the way to Devon one Christmas holiday. Our Christmas presents were packed in a big box on the roof-rack. I remember Dad breaking the ice on a ditch beside the road, scooping up some muddy water and pouring it into the radiator. Soon we were on our way again as though nothing had happened. Dad was a very practical man, brilliant at DIY and an engineer at heart. Mum first knew she was in love with him when the band's car broke down on the way to a concert. Dad popped open the bonnet and fixed it.

Dad was a teacher. We had very little money, but we never went hungry. Our parents must have been very careful with the little they had, because it couldn't have been easy feeding so many growing children. I often helped Dad in the garden, where he grew an abundance of fruit and vegetables. Christmas was always a happy time, and our presents were carefully and lovingly chosen. It was made very clear to us that the joy of Christmas was giving, not receiving. I remember being given my first watch. It was digital and had an inbuilt timer function. I loved to set it as I left the school gates, racing home as fast as I could go. Each day I tried to beat my time. When it was stolen from a changing room at the local swimming pool I was inconsolable.

Home was also quite a strict place. It would have been chaotic growing up in a house full of children unless there were rules. My father brought his classroom discipline home and we always knew the boundaries, which is a good thing for a young child. There was no cable TV or videos to watch, and computer games were only just becoming affordable for some households, but certainly not ours, so we made our own fun. I have many happy memories of putting on plays and puppet shows for the adults with my brothers, sisters and cousins, or playing card and board games.

TV was rationed: each of us was given ten marbles a week and each marble could be "spent" on one TV programme. I often spent mine on the first day and then had to leave the lounge each time one of my brothers or sisters, who carefully rationed their marbles over the entire week, wanted to watch their favourite shows. I never got to watch *Dr Who* – not because it was too scary, but it was on Saturday evening and I just didn't have any marbles left. I showed similar behaviour during school holidays when, in an experiment to teach us to manage our money, we were each given £5 to last the week and we had to cater for ourselves. My sisters all bought rice and vegetables and had plenty to eat. I ran out of money on day two. I still can't eat Mars Bars to this day!

Although our home was a loving place, I must have pushed my dad close to the edge on several occasions. Once during a long Christmas holiday, I did something so terrible that my dad chased me through the house. Cornered, I fell to the floor and my dad kicked me so hard that he broke a bone in his foot. We all thought it was hilarious. It's still a family joke to this day. I was often beaten with a hairbrush, but never with the hard side. The hairbrush also became a legend in our family. "I'll take the hairbrush to you!" was the ultimate threat and usually worked to calm me down. I must have been a real handful and it would have been difficult to constantly correct me with five other children to contend with. My parents were probably at their wits' end about how to discipline me.

Even though we were known locally as the "Larcombe Clan", I never felt as though there was a shortage of love to go round. Nevertheless, one-to-one time with either of our parents was a rare treat to be savoured, as it was with our grandparents. I was eight years old when, one August day, Dad decided I needed a special talking to. We set off on an adventure to Lyme Regis on the Dorset coast. The journey would give my father time to talk to me and try to instil some discipline. He took me fishing for mackerel on a little boat and I loved every minute. On the way home, he told me that if he saw me pulling my sister's hair, or being disruptive, he would just say the word "mackerel". I don't think it worked, but it was one of the best days of my life up to that point and demonstrates how little time I shared exclusively with my father.

In order to miss a day at school, we had to be seriously ill. And I mean close to death! Once a great game of "war" developed at school, which soon spread to the adventure playground. I "realistically died" by falling out of a tree-house, having been "shot" by the enemy. The headmaster put my arm in a sling and sent me home. Unfortunately for me, it was April Fool's Day and Mum just did not believe I was hurt. The next morning I was still in pain and my arm had turned a nasty shade of purple. Reluctantly she took me to hospital, where we discovered that my wrist was broken in two places. It was the first of several visits my mother and I made to Accident and Emergency. I broke a number of different bones and it became a joke between us every time the triage nurse at reception asked if it was my first visit to A & E!

I had my revenge one April Fool's Day a few years later when I called Mum from school.

"Mum, it's me. I've had an accident at school. They think my arm may be broken. It definitely needs a visit to the hospital."

When she arrived looking very worried, I slipped on a sling and walked out to the car, holding my bandaged elbow. I will never forget the look of relief on her face when, halfway to hospital, I ripped off the bandage and shouted, "April Fool!"

I felt a special bond with my mother, who somehow understood my bad behaviour differently to my father. I am certain young people can achieve anything as long as those around them believe in them too. Parents and particularly teachers have the power to set the young free to exceed their dreams or to crush them comprehensively. I am convinced that my later successes were due to my mother's constant belief in me.

CHAPTER 4

Saying Goodbye

About a year after Otty died, I came back from school early one day and was surprised to see my dad at home. He was now a teaching adviser in nearby Tunbridge Wells and never usually got home before 7 p.m.

"Where's Mum?" I asked.

"She's not so well; she's just gone to lie down for a few hours."

The few hours lasted for thirty-eight days, before eventually she was taken into hospital. In her early twenties, Mum had been diagnosed with encephalitis, an acute inflammation of the brain and the membranes that surround it, usually caused by a viral infection. Although she made a full recovery then, the virus had lain dormant and now she was showing all the same symptoms.

For me, her illness marked the end of my childhood, the end of happy family times where cares and troubles are things your parents shoulder for you. My dad tried so hard to protect us from the truth that she was seriously ill. He gave everything to try to keep up our routines, our clubs and our normality. By then I was swimming at quite a high level in age-group competitions, which meant early-morning training five days a week, plus four evenings and most weekends.

Sarah was ten years older than my youngest brother Richard. This spread of ages meant we attended different schools. The effort of getting us all ready, feeding us and washing and pressing different school uniforms, as well as nursing a seriously ill wife, must have sapped all Dad's strength before he even arrived at work. I don't ever remember an occasion when he did anything for himself other than read the *Daily Telegraph* in bed before he went to sleep.

People were very kind, bringing a succession of meals and offering to look after us. I often went to stay with friends for weeks on end, not really understanding why. We all grew up very quickly, but my sister Sarah, at the age of fourteen, made the biggest step of all, taking Mum's place by organizing us, ensuring we had packed lunches each morning and overseeing bath time in the evening for the younger ones. Because Sarah took such a key role, she became very close to my dad. Each evening they sat down to plan the next day. It couldn't have been much fun, but I felt a little resentful at their closeness.

I was too young to really understand why our idyllic life had to end so abruptly. My concept of illness was a tummy bug that lasted, at worst, two days. I'd learned from Mum that illness had to be ignored while life carried on. So I kept thinking Mum would be home soon and our lives could return to normal. After my first hospital visit, I realized life would never be the same again.

While other parents kissed their children goodbye as they were dropped at the school gate, I grew used to being dropped off two miles away so Dad could avoid the traffic and still make it to his office on time. Inside, I missed being kissed, but I couldn't show it. Everyone else was being so brave; I hated to let the side down. I wanted my mum, not my sister, to wash my cuts. I kept pestering my dad for the chance to visit.

When Mum was moved from a special hospital in London to the hospital in Tunbridge Wells, Dad finally gave in to my constant requests.

"She's going to be really sleepy, so don't expect too much. Don't sit on the bed and don't talk too loudly," my dad warned me as we drove the seven miles through a heavy April shower. The shower soon passed and the spring sun was shining as we parked the car outside the bleak-looking hospital. I was so happy to be able to see

Mum again. I couldn't wait to give her a big hug and tell her how much I missed her.

There was nothing Dad could have said that would have sufficiently prepared me for that first visit. Mum had her own room. The nerve cells in her spinal column had become dangerously inflamed and any light or sound caused her great pain. The curtains in her room were closed tightly. When my eyes had adjusted to the gloom, it wasn't my mother I saw. All I could focus on were the plastic tubes coming out of a thin person's nose and the saline drip that fed into a bruised stick that had once been my mother's wrist. She was wearing a big pair of dark glasses. When she spoke it reminded me of Otty's last day. It was only fifteen months since Otty's funeral and I still missed her.

I don't really remember what I said or what Mum said to me. I just remember a feeling of hopelessness as I trudged back to the car through endless corridors. The sanitary smell of disinfectant filled my nostrils, making me feel sick. This was the hospital where Mum and I had so often waited while some broken part of my body was either X-rayed or re-set. It was a place where Mum brought me to get mended. Now she was the broken one and there was nothing I could do to fix her.

It started to rain again on our way home and the wipers were barely able to keep the windscreen clear. Dad had something to tell me. "I've spoken to Sarah, but the others don't know yet. I put the house on the market last week."

"What do you mean?" I asked, dreading the answer.

"It's just too much to keep living in the country. We're going to move back to town." I looked out at the green fields and the hedgerows. A little part of me died. The world was a tough place after all.

In no time, the open fields, the woods and the freedom of life in the country were exchanged or a terraced house with a paved back garden ten metres long by five metres wide. I didn't want to lose all my friends, so I stayed on at the same school, catching a bus each morning for the nine-mile trip back over the border to East Sussex. Dad bought me a bike and I cycled each morning and evening to the swimming pool, rain or shine. And I learned to be more self-reliant.

About a year later, tired from evening swimming training, I was reading in my bedroom. There was a knock on my door, and Dad came in and sat at the end of my bed. He looked completely drained; his eyes were red. I suspected he'd been crying. I'd never seen him cry before.

"Just, I think you are old enough for me to tell you this, but, other than Sarah, your brothers and sisters don't know what I'm about to tell you." He paused to compose himself; I could see how hard it was for him. This wasn't the first time he had started a conversation with words like those. I didn't like it the first time and I suspected I wasn't going to like it now.

"I have just left your mother in the hospital. It's quite bad. The doctors have told me to be prepared for the possibility that she won't last through the night. They've given her some medication that she may or may not respond to. I sat with her just now and said goodbye. I want you to be prepared for the worst."

I cried through most of the night, remembering the times Mum had picked me up when I had fallen over, the laughter and the love. She was always there for me. I was fourteen, but that night I felt as though I had grown up by ten years. I was face to face with the likelihood of enormous loss, and the feeling was one of total helplessness.

It would be almost thirty years before I again faced such loss, felt so helpless and cried so uncontrollably.

CHAPTER 5

Channelling My Energy

Mum responded to the drugs and came home. Although she was either bed-bound or confined to a wheelchair, depending on the cycle of her relapse and recovery, I still had her with me. Having said goodbye to her, I saw every day she lived as a bonus.

I have very happy memories of my senior school years. Although Mum was still seriously ill, we just got on with life as a family. Mum was very determined to get well and act as though everything was quite normal. When others fussed over her and insisted she rest, I was happy to treat her as normal. Uncle Justyn bought her an electric wheelchair that we christened "the Bug". While other members of my family were embarrassed at being seen in town with this rather eccentric lady who used to whizz about at full speed, I just loved going out with her for zips around the park or down to the supermarket for the weekly shop, accompanied by her constant companion, a little Jack Russell called Minty. We had a lift installed in the house, and a series of ramps and rails were fitted so she could get around the three-storey town-house.

One of the side-effects of Mum's illness was that she had no feeling in her hands. Although by this time we had an almost full-time home help to cook and clean for us, when Mum felt well enough she always wanted to get back in the kitchen and look after us all. While others told her to lie back down, I used to love Mum's determination.

One day, towards the end of a summer term, the bus broke down on the way home and by the time I got back, I was ravenous.

I found Mum in the kitchen. I was too late for supper, but she had put my dinner in the oven and while I made a cup of tea she opened the oven door to get the food out. There was a sizzling noise. I turned round to see Mum lifting a red-hot dish with her bare hands! She felt no pain, but there was a distinct smell that had nothing to do with my food. Suddenly I wasn't hungry any more. Despite her blistered hands, we turned the incident into a joke. Another source of hilarity was when she got her words jumbled up. Sometimes the sentences she came out with were really rather rude!

In her book *Journey into God's Heart* (Hodder & Stoughton, 2006) Mum talks about this time in her life as being quite hard. While she was away in hospital, we learned to adapt and built coping strategies without her. Our lives had moved on and Mum had to re-establish her role in the family. I accepted that she was just a bit different and adjusted very quickly. She was my mum and I was always going to love her.

At school I was doing well. I loved any sport, but I excelled at swimming. Swimming taught me the discipline I lacked as a child. It gave me the focus I needed and helped me to concentrate academically. I had no excess energy to burn off doing mischief. I learned to wake myself before six each morning, cycle to the pool, swim for an hour, and catch the bus to school and back. I had an hour or two to do my homework before training again in the evening. Then I did the whole thing again the next day.

At weekends I represented my club or county anywhere in the UK or even further afield in international open meets in Europe and North America. One evening, half-way through a training session, my club coach Mick and assistant coach Ted took me to one side. I was worried I'd done something wrong, or was going to get a telling off for my lack of application.

Mick Geer wore pressed trousers and a perfect white polo shirt. He always seemed to have a tan, and none of his short grey hairs were ever out of place. He smelled of aftershave and wore a chunky gold watch on his wrist and a matching chain round his neck. Mick was one of the best swimming coaches in the country and had coached more than one Olympian. He went on to be appointed Head Coach of the British Paralympic Swimming team at the Sydney Olympic Games.

By appearance, Ted was the complete opposite: a lovable rogue, he had scruffy blond hair and a shaggy beard. He always wore trunks that showed off his builder's bottom. Both coaches demanded and were given complete respect from their loyal swimmers. They both looked very serious as they sat me down on a poolside bench, but when Mick used my nickname, I knew I wasn't in trouble.

"Lord Larcombe, Ted and I both agree, you have the ability to go all the way. If you want it enough, it's there to be taken, but you have to really want it."

I really wanted it and that year I smashed the club and county records and won the Southern County Championships in three different strokes. After one swim, a 50m sprint in the Olympic Pool at Crystal Palace, I couldn't understand why Mick looked so happy.

"Hey, Lordy, you've only gone and broken the bloody Junior European record!" Mick said as he affectionately put me in a headlock! Dad hadn't been able to come and I was disappointed that he'd missed that moment. I didn't have much of a chance to celebrate, because someone else swam even faster in the next heat.

I made a lot of sacrifices for my sport, because I wanted to be the best. The biggest competition of the year, the National Age Groups, always took place in the summer holidays. It meant I never really had the freedom of a summer holiday in my teenage years; I was always in full-time training. That meant a minimum of twelve hours a week. Unlike my school friends, I didn't go to parties because I was always travelling at weekends. Besides, I had a strict diet to stick to, so there was never a temptation to drink or smoke. Temptation just wasn't an issue.

Although I made sacrifices, swimming gave so much back to me. I applied the same discipline and hard work to my studies at school. My sister Sarah is incredibly intelligent. She went up to Oxford and achieved the highest mark for her History degree. Not content with a degree, she stayed on to complete her Masters before being invited to join the academic staff. While I excelled on the sporting field, I had to work hard academically. Luckily, I was good at hard work. What I lacked in academic flair, I made up for in graft.

Another factor driving me forward at school was my unrelenting desire to become a pilot. I achieved some of the best results in my school in the final year of "O" Levels before they became GCSEs. Someone told me I needed Maths and Physics at "A" Level to be a pilot. These were my weakest subjects, but I had achieved good "O" Level grades, so the school supported me when I decided to do Maths and Physics at "A" Level, as well as the subjects I was good at like Geography, Biology and Art. Looking back now, it was a huge amount to take on academically, especially as I was still competing in the pool and indulging my dream of flying by signing up for the Air Cadets. There was talk of me being made Head Boy. To top it all, I was awarded a Sixth Form scholarship by the RAF to support me financially through my "A" Level studies. Perhaps I would have managed it all if the school hadn't opened its doors to girls. Something had to give! The next two years of my life did not go according to plan.

Temptation first entered my disciplined life in the form of a beautiful girl called Sasha. Full of fun, she made my swimming records, my aircraft magazines and even my studies seem dull in comparison. My obsession with Sasha exerted an irresistible force on me like none I'd ever experienced. Mesmerized by her beauty, I found myself volunteering for classes I had no interest in or making friends with her classmates just so they might say nice things about me to Sasha. I even calculated where she would be at any point in the day, just so I could pass by in the opposite direction as often as I could.

When we became boyfriend and girlfriend, I suddenly realized how square I was, how untrendy and how *good*. I was studying for four "A" levels, as well as other higher-level exams; I was still swimming each morning, and in the evenings I either did more swimming or attended Air Cadets, which involved a fourteen-mile bike trip twice a week. My weekends were taken up by competitions.

Sasha opened my eyes to many things the other, cooler people in my year had already experienced through parties and experimentation. Now I too wanted to attend social events and parties. Completely smitten by her, I neglected my friends, my studies and my swimming. I was exhausted; by juggling everything in the air, I found myself being good at nothing. Eventually, something had to change. In the end, making the choice to stop swimming was the only sensible thing to do. My times were not really getting any faster. One morning my alarm hammered out its annoying bleep at 5.30 a.m. I tried to open my eyes, but for the first time, I fell back to sleep, oblivious as the alarm continued to shriek.

I missed training and even had to run for the school bus. That was when I realized I just didn't have the desire to go through the pain barrier any more day in, day out. It was still a very hard decision and I dreaded telling my coaches Mick and Ted. They had been like fathers to me; in fact, I probably spent more time with them than with my own dad. They had watched me as I grew up from a hyperactive eleven-year-old to a much more serious teenager. They had travelled with me around the world, picked me up when I was down and shared all the successes. They were a formidable team and I had always obediently followed their instructions. Now a gangly seventeen-year-old, a constant in their successful club side, I had to break the news. I wasn't looking forward to it.

They didn't take the news well and, for several years, I carried with me a feeling that I had failed them. I realized that my motivation for swimming over the last year had been a desire not to let them down. They had invested so much time and effort in me. I found it really difficult to walk away. They persuaded me not to give up completely and I agreed to go on competing, but I cut down on the swimming training. For me this had a bad effect. Although on the outside I seemed confident and I was physically stronger than my schoolmates, on the inside I was insecure. I needed to feel I was liked and accepted, and I needed the reassurance that winning competitions had given me. Now that I wasn't training, I stopped winning. I felt I was letting everyone down.

My dad had also made huge sacrifices to support my competitive swimming. When we had lived in the country, he got up early every morning to drive me to the pool. I made the mistake of not consulting him before I told the coaches. In my pride I hadn't considered how he would feel about me turning my back on a sport in which I had shown such talent. I know it hurt him a great deal. I hadn't considered that he loved his trips round the country with the other parents, supporting the club. He helped with the coaching on Monday nights and had made new friends. I will never forget the look of sadness on his face as we journeyed home together from my last club gala in Guildford. I sat next to him on the team bus, but he wouldn't speak to me all the way back. When we did finally discuss it, I realized he thought the reason for my "giving up" was to spend more time with Sasha. I was cross and denied it, but he was probably right.

But all was not going well on that front. Sasha liked me all the time I had another interest, a focus other than her. She liked it when I won races and sometimes, if the events were local, she came to watch me compete. But now, the novelty of going out with the school sports captain was wearing off. I sensed she was getting bored, and the harder I tried, the worse it became. I thought I could impress her with gifts and sophisticated meals at restaurants. However, the money I was due to receive from the RAF for the scholarship had yet to arrive. I was about to do one of the most foolish things I ever did in my young life.

It was the summer term of 1986 and the school fancy dress ball was just a week away. Over the last month, we had been carefully painting scenery in our art class and now the decorations were going up. There was a buzz of excitement in the sixth-form common room, but I was in a bit of a conundrum. I had nothing to wear. I wanted a gangster outfit from the fancy dress shop, but I couldn't afford to hire it. I asked my dad for a loan. He knew the money for the scholarship was coming, so he very kindly agreed and advanced me the entire first instalment. I was so happy at the time. However, perhaps this incident made me believe in easy, instant money. What need was there to save?

The romance didn't last. However, free from any distraction, I knuckled down to my studies and just about scraped the grades I needed for college. Just before the end of my final term, an official-looking light-blue letter arrived. I knew who it was from because the crest of the Royal Air Force was printed on the back. I had been called forward to attend their selection centre. The course of my life was about to change.

Chapter 6

Free-falling

The heat was stifling as I arrived at the gates of RAF Biggin Hill, dressed in my one and only suit. It had been a long walk from the station and now my shirt was drenched. I loosened the knot of my tie and shifted the weight of my bag to my other shoulder. I could smell the tarmac melting in the sweltering August sun. My shoes were sticky as I walked the last hundred metres to the imposing guardroom. I knew most of the nearby RAF bases from my time as a cadet. Biggin Hill, on top of the North Downs and just to the south of London, had been a key base during the Battle of Britain.

I had no ambition to go to university. I knew I could never compete with Sarah. All I wanted to do was become a fast jet pilot, my passion for planes having continued since those early model aircraft. You don't have to be academically brilliant to fly, but you do need the ability to think fast under pressure. The RAF has perfected a three-day selection process to identify whether or not an individual possesses the physical and mental aptitude required to be a pilot.

I was told to wait in the shade of the guardroom and soon I was joined by other hopeful and very nervous young men, dressed almost identically to me and looking equally uncomfortable. We were led to a large hut which contained row upon row of metal-framed beds, communal showers at one end and toilets at the other.

Over the course of three days, I endured being prodded and poked with sticks and little hammers to test my reflexes. My hearing and eyesight were checked, and I sat through so many interviews, I lost count after the second day.

After three days we all gathered in a large room. On the walls hung aviation prints, as though we needed reminding of why we were there. I could feel the tension and we all laughed heartily at the slightest opportunity. It felt like an age before a smartly uniformed officer with a huge moustache walked in and called out a few names. My name wasn't one of them. As the named men were led out of the room, I assumed they were being dismissed, and felt sorry for them. The rest of us were invited to stay seated. I never contemplated the prospect of failure. All my dreams were shattered as we were told we hadn't made it through. I hadn't achieved a good enough score in my aptitude tests for consideration as aircrew, but they invited me to apply for a ground role in a year's time and suggested I go to college. They told me I could even re-take my aptitude tests and have another try in a few years. Although devastated, I was immediately determined to find another way to achieve my lifetime ambition.

However, as I didn't immediately identify another way, I felt as though I had jumped into thin air. I was in a kind of free-fall. I landed, more by accident than by planning, at teacher training college, specializing in PE. It was the same college my father and my great-grandfather had once attended in West London. As Mum and Dad drove me to the Twickenham campus, I noticed that the trees looked tired and ready for autumn. After advice, tears and kisses, they left, and that was it. I was eighteen years old and I was on my own.

I didn't really enjoy college. It felt like a transition rather than a destination. I became restless in my final year. I kept thinking I was marking time until I was let out into the real world. I just wanted to re-sit my aptitude test and start flying training. But those years were not all bad. I discovered I loved playing rugby and jumping out of aeroplanes.

Being a student generally means being poor. My friends all had jobs washing pots in hotels or serving burgers in fast-food restaurants. But after my first term, I saw an advertisement in the student bar and applied to join one of the Army's Reserve Parachute Battalions. Selection was intense. Every weekend for six weeks I travelled down to Wales in an old Bedford lorry and humped a heavy pack across the Brecon Beacons while my fellow students drank their way through their student grants. Selection culminated in a tough two-week selection camp held at the headquarters of the regular Army's elite Parachute Regiment in Aldershot. At the end of the course, the few of us that remained had earned the right to wear the coveted red beret. But this was just the pre-selection course for the main event – the opportunity to attend the RAF's Military Parachute Training School.

I still have a photo of the day I was awarded my red beret. I'm smiling, but both my eyes are swollen and bruised from one of the military tests known as milling. This involves sixty seconds of uncontrolled aggression in a boxing ring. My opponent was a very large and streetwise Cockney who landed a lot of punches! But I did well. The photo shows me being awarded the Champion Recruit's Trophy, a silver beer tankard which saw much use over the coming years.

While I enjoyed the selection course, the actual parachute training, on the other hand, was one of the most terrifying experiences of my life. Military parachuting is not at all like sports parachuting or skydiving, both of which I have enjoyed. Military parachutes are not steerable; they fall through the air very quickly and you are thrown out of fast-flying aircraft at frighteningly low levels with up to eighty other people at the same time in full equipment, at night and sometimes over water. The aim is to keep vulnerable time in the air as short as possible, reducing the chance of being shot at. However, it does lead to a huge number of quite horrific jump injuries, some of which I witnessed first-hand.

My first jump involved going up in a little basket below a hot-air balloon with five other white-faced recruits. I was last to go and I can safely say that I have never been more scared in my life. It didn't help when the person before me refused to throw himself over the side and had to be unstrapped. If this happens when you are fully trained, it's a court-martial offence.

I had no intention of throwing away all the hard graft I had put in to get to where I was, so over the side I went, feeling as if I had just jumped in front of a train in the hope that the driver would see me and apply the brakes in time to stop. As my canopy opened above me, I felt total relief and realized why milling is a good test. Deliberately jumping into thin air is an act of complete aggression, preferably not involving the use of the brain.

It was a Sunday evening in my third year at college. I had just arrived back from a reservist training weekend and all I wanted was a bath and my bed. There was a note on the door of my room at the student hall of residence. I'd missed a call from my sister Naomie and the message told me to call her. It said, *Urgent – about Mum.* I changed out of my smelly combat kit, grabbed some coins and went down to the lobby to join the queue for the communal payphone.

I wondered what could be wrong. Mum's life had been gathering momentum while I was away. Her buggy had given her so much mobility that she travelled around more than any of the family, accepting invitations to speak at ladies' breakfasts and other gatherings. In her late teens, probably inspired by Otty, she had written several books that went to print. There was never time to write while she was bringing us all up, but while confined to bed, she used the time to write with a little electronic typewriter. A publisher encouraged her to share what it was like to raise a family of six children after being struck down by such a debilitating illness.

The story seemed to resonate with many and Mum became a bit of a celebrity in certain circles. Her regular magazine articles in *Family* and other publications were well received. Any of us who were close to hand could help load the Bug into the back of the car, and Dad or a friend then drove Mum to wherever in the country she was speaking. When she got back, exhausted, the Bug would be unloaded and Mum would be carried up to her bedroom. Although it would take her a day or two to recover each time, nothing ever put Mum off. I don't think she's refused many invitations to speak, regardless of the location anywhere in the British Isles and even further afield.

"She's *what?*" I couldn't believe my ears when I finally called home and spoke to my youngest sister.

"She literally got home and picked up her wheelchair and carried it up the steps! I was there. I saw the whole thing. She was giggling like a child!"

Normally I would have just laughed it off, but Naomie is probably the most sensible of all the Larcombe children. It wasn't something she'd make up. I think I jumped for joy. There were four people waiting for the phone by the time I put the receiver down. I got some very strange looks.

I phoned home every day for the next week, just to check Mum was still mobile. Her story is stunning and it had the top medical experts in the country scratching their heads. She records what happened that day in her book *Unexpected Healing* (Hodder & Stoughton, 1989).

During my final year at college, I met someone who was about to join the Army Air Corps. He too had failed his aptitude tests for an RAF fast-jet pilot, but had been accepted to train as a helicopter pilot with the Army. At that time, just after the first Gulf War, the Army Air Corps was about to take delivery of the US-built Apache anti-tank helicopter. That was good enough for me! I applied and, after a further three days of testing at the Army's Regular Commissions Board, I received the letter I longed for. It informed me that I had been accepted for officer training and was "respectfully requested" to report to the Royal Military Academy, Sandhurst, that coming September. There was a long list of kit items I needed to bring and a very strict dress code to adhere to. Best of all, there was no need to attend any further selection for flying training. My marks in the RAF aptitude test were good enough for the Army Air Corps. I celebrated long and hard. My beer tankard still has the dents to prove it.

My final exams couldn't come quickly enough. The day finally arrived when, dressed in a smart navy-blue blazer and grey flannel trousers and duly armed with an ironing board, I reported to a huge concrete building known as Victory College. The building, nicknamed "the Bunker", had won an award for innovative design in the sixties. All around me were hundreds of young men in blazers and grey flannel trousers wandering about with big ironing boards tucked under their arms. I was no longer a civilian: my military career had begun, and somehow my life was back on track. I had landed.

PART 2

The Army

He who has felt the deepest grief is best able to experience supreme happiness.

ALEXANDRE DUMAS

CHAPTER 7

Blade Running

Officer training at Sandhurst is one of the world's most respected military leadership courses. Countries from all around the world pay for the privilege of sending their future kings and generals to be educated there. The mantra for survival at Sandhurst is to become a "grey man". Never do anything badly and absolutely never do anything well, for fear of drawing attention to yourself.

I drew attention to myself on the third day of term. Sandhurst had a strong rugby team. Officer cadets are confined to barracks for the first five weeks under curfew and a strictly enforced zero-alcohol regime. There was a strong rumour that those lucky enough to be selected for the Academy First Fifteen were able to share a few pints in the bar after the matches every Wednesday and Saturday. These matches took precedence over all other training. The rugby trials were scheduled for Saturday and Sunday of the first week. It seemed to me that the whole intake of 410 officer cadets turned out to secure their place.

I played well on Saturday and was told to report back for final selection the following day. But my faith had grown quite strong by that time and I decided it was important for me to keep Sundays special. So I did the unthinkable. I declined the invitation and went to chapel instead. Although it was unheard of for a cadet to refuse to do something they were told to do, Sandhurst encourages free thinking, and personal integrity is highly regarded. My decision was respected. Although I didn't make the starting team who were selected to play that coming Wednesday, I did make it to the reserve bench.

It was agony watching the game unfold from the sideline. I was desperate for a chance to get on the pitch and spent the first twenty minutes running up and down the touchline to make sure I was warmed up, and to remind the coach I was keen. Suddenly there was a loud blast of the whistle and our team medic ran onto the pitch.

"Take your tracksuit off, Larcombe – you're on!" the coach shouted. My tracksuit was already off. I felt pure exhilaration as I ran onto the pitch. *This is my chance*! I thought. I was so determined to make a good impression, I played out of my skin, tackled like a demon and scored two tries. The following Saturday I made the starting line-up. The week after I was made the captain. I didn't miss a single game for the whole season.

The Academy commandant is a very senior general; few officer cadets ever get to meet him. However, the commandant when I was at Sandhurst was keen on his rugby and watched all our home matches, come rain or shine. Captaining a side of leaders was a huge honour for me and the team was successful, losing only two matches in the entire season, which included victories against the US Officer Academy as well as the RAF and Royal Navy Academies.

From the day of the rugby trial, I was never going to be a grey man. Not only was I rugby captain, but I was entitled and expected to wear my military parachute badge on my right arm, a mark of someone who has already completed one of the toughest military selection courses in the Army. My fitness, and the fact that I had previous military experience, meant that my card was marked.

On the first day of the final term a list was posted on the noticeboard of our accommodation block. Officer cadets at Sandhurst live under constant scrutiny. Each cadet in the intake is graded, from the top performer to the lowest. If you're in the bottom half you know you stand a chance of being "chopped", and it's back to civilian life very quickly. In the top group, you have a chance of being awarded the Sword of Honour: you are a "Blade Runner". Being in the middle is a good thing because you don't face the risk of being chopped, but you also don't get the added pressure of being in the spotlight all the time. If you have performed well, during the final term you are awarded a cadet rank. These ranks vary depending on how you are doing.

Before I had the chance to read the list, cadets from the two rooms next to me squeezed themselves into my cupboard that passed itself off as a room and the banter started up. I was still unpacking my kit bag after the brief holiday.

"Hey, Blade, good Christmas? I hope you're not going to start bossing us around now you're all important!" said one of them.

"Don't forget your mates!" said another.

As I studied the list of cadet ranks I felt a huge sense of achievement at the letters "JUO" next to my name. Junior under officer was the highest rank at that stage. There were only four JUOs out of 400 cadets and the likelihood was that one of them would go on to be granted the rank of senior under officer and be awarded the Sword of Honour. I felt my pulse racing because I also knew I was going to be tested. There would be extra duties, and on every test and exercise I would be given additional "command appointments", meaning I had to sit up through the night writing orders for a dawn attack, while my fellow cadets got their heads down. All the senior directing staff, or "DS", as they were known, would arrive just before I gave my orders, to assess the quality (or otherwise) of my plan, the level of detail and the confidence of my delivery.

Cadets are divided into units, or platoons, of about thirty. This is the standard fighting unit in an infantry battalion. If a platoon is unlucky enough to have a "Blade Runner" in their midst, it usually means they all have to work harder and get less sleep, as the "lucky" cadet is put in situations where he can be tested. For me, this meant I became quite unpopular with my fellow cadets and it became a bit of a joke, as every time the "top brass" turned up when we were on exercise, it meant something was about to "kick off". However, for our platoon commander and platoon sergeant (our instructors from the serving Army), it was quite an honour and it reflected well on them if they had a "Blade" in their group.

Late on a very wet evening in February, out on exercise, I had just suspended my plastic poncho between two trees in a vain attempt to keep dry and was trying to get a few hours' sleep, when an order was passed to me by a soaking wet radio sentry. We had already spent several days in the field and were all exhausted from a day spent humping our packs across the wet mountains. The order was to set an ambush by first light. Struggling in the darkness and the rain, I wrote my orders and successfully led the platoon to their ambush positions without being located by the "enemy" – a company of highly trained Gurkhas. I set both cut-off groups on one side of a track above and below the place where I expected the enemy to arrive at some point over the next six hours. Once satisfied with the positioning, I returned to the killing group in the centre of our formation. The signal for the platoon to spring the ambush would be the sound of my light support weapon opening up on full automatic. If I did not open fire, even if there were possible enemy in our sights, no one else was to open fire.

After several hours of waiting in a cold and very wet ditch in the Brecon Beacons, I gently rested my head on the rear sight of my rifle and closed my eyes as huge drops of Welsh rain rolled off my helmet and down my heavily painted face. The next thing I knew was a sharp pain in my thigh. I looked up to see our platoon sergeant instructor just before a second hefty kick landed on my leg. Seeing I now had his full attention, he nodded over to the track where I could see six or more menacing-looking Gurkhas walking right through my killing area. I squeezed the trigger, firing at least ten rounds of blank ammunition in one long burst. All hell broke loose, with the rest of my platoon joining in and throwing smoke and simulated grenades onto the track. Having successfully set and executed the ambush, we all crashed back to the pre-agreed rendezvous point.

Until the writing of this book, only my instructor and I knew how close I had come to sleeping through the ambush. If I'd failed, I would certainly have dropped out of the race for the coveted Sword.

The final exercise, the culmination of all our training, provided the last chance to decide our overall grading. We flew off to the island of Cyprus, where Greek and Turkish Cypriots fought each other in the late sixties. A ruined village which had seen the most ferocious battle now formed part of a Military Training Area and was to be the scene of our final attack – an attack I had the honour of planning and leading, directing the action of all 400 cadets. One of the highlights was to be an afternoon training with Rigid Raider Assault Craft, high-speed inflatable boats with huge engines and rigid floors.

The sea swell was at the upper extreme for operation, but the decision was made to take us out in small groups. I never got the opportunity for a turn. A wave flipped two of the boats in the group beforehand, throwing the cadets and instructors into the sea. As they scrambled onto one of the upturned boats, another wave lifted the other boat and dropped it on the first, crushing one of the cadets. He died later that same day from internal injuries. It was a harsh lesson to learn that military training, if it is going to be effective, can never be risk free. I was reminded of this several years later when, on exercise in Canada, my unit was accidentally mortared by our own troops.

Back in the UK, training completed, we were waiting at the side of the drill square before our first rehearsal for the traditional Sovereign's Parade, when we would finally graduate. There was a buzz of excitement: the end was in sight and the final awards were about to be announced, including the promotion of one cadet to senior under officer, the recipient of the Sword. My platoon staff sergeant came over and took me for some extra drill and taught me the protocol for accepting a sword from royalty. He winked at me. It was the best wink I ever received from a man! I think he was even more proud than I was.

My military career had started well. Receiving the Sword, which had already been engraved with my name, was the proudest day of my life. I felt I was on top of the world. But I was about to return to earth with a bump.

CHAPTER 8

Down to Earth

As I drove past the guardroom at the Headquarters of the Army Air Corps in Middle Wallop, Hampshire, on a cool but sunny day in late May, I was reminded of the day I reported for selection at RAF Biggin Hill. In contrast to my scruffy suit, I now proudly wore the uniform of a junior officer. In terms of experience I was as green as the freshly cut grass I could smell by the runway, and I knew next to nothing of the realities of military life. I soon realized there was a lot to learn.

On our first day we were formally welcomed by a senior officer, but reminded that until we learned to fly, we were a waste of rations. He also told us that it was likely that half of us in the room would fail our flying course. I looked around, desperately hoping to be one of the successes.

The first part of flying training is quite ruthless. Military pilots have to pick things up quickly, because the cost of training a pilot is huge. Aspiring pilots need to learn at the right pace, or face the chop. Each evening in the mess we student pilots shared our notes, each trying to outdo the other with our exploits, as though we were veteran aviators. I had little to say during these conversations, not out of modesty, but because I genuinely realized I was not achieving my flying goals at the same pace as the others. While I was more than comfortable taking off and actually quite good in the air, I had a fundamental problem. I could not for the life of me land the stupid plane. The harder I tried, the worse I got. I ended up just doing circuit after circuit in the forlorn hope of finding the elusive formula of the correct angle of approach, airspeed and application of flap that was required.

My instructor was becoming almost as frustrated as I was. "Set everything up right, well ahead of time, and she'll land herself." I was too busy trying to force the thing down on the deck. I was living my dream and discovering it was actually a nightmare, but I was not going to let a silly little thing like landing destroy my lifelong ambition of flight.

I woke early on the last day of the initial ten-hour fixed-wing course, known as Flying Grading. I knew this was it – one last chance to make the grade. I felt physically sick and couldn't manage breakfast. I had spent much of the night rehearsing all the things I had to do in the final circuit, and now I felt hung over. I knew what I had to do, I just had to do it this time. The pressure was immense.

Things were looking quite good as I brought the little Chipmunk Mark 2 gently round on the last leg of the circuit. I extended the flaps, re-trimmed the aircraft and applied just the right amount of throttle to allow the aircraft to settle down to its final approach. Even my final turn into wind was looking good and I dabbed at the rudder pedals like any professional to keep the nose pointing straight. But then it all started to go wrong.

Instead of trusting the aircraft to glide down its final approach path, I tried to force it onto the grass strip, but the nose kept bobbing up, then down as I overcorrected. I had to play with the throttle in response to a violent shudder, a warning that the onset of a stall was not far away; any stall would be fatal at this height. I wrestled with the aircraft, cursing the torque from the engine that was driving me sideways. I hit the deck hard with a sickening crunch and bounced so high I ran out of runway. Following the correct drill, I quickly applied full power to get out of the circuit and try again. I was so concerned with getting my speed right that I didn't look outside the cockpit. Suddenly I felt the controls pull violently in my hands as my instructor, sitting behind me, wrestled to avoid a collision with another aircraft in the circuit. I was close enough to the other plane to see the trainee pilot's face and recognize the terror in his eyes. I also saw the angry hand gesture of his instructor as we flew over the top of them, missing them by inches. Our little aircraft was buffeted by the slipstream.

After each sortie, your instructor takes you to one side and goes over every part of the flight, picking out good and bad. This time, once he had landed the aircraft, my instructor, now white as a sheet, just left me in the cockpit and staggered towards the hangar.

That afternoon we were all called in to see the officer commanding the Flying Training School. I was one of the last in line. Most of the other interviews took five minutes or even longer. Mine lasted little more than a minute. I'll never forget his words. "We've carefully considered your ability. It might be a good idea to find an alternative occupation to flying, before you kill yourself or someone else."

That experience brought me down to earth. I had a choice: I could leave the Army now, or find another regiment to join. It didn't take me long to decide. I liked the Army and therefore chose another regiment. If I couldn't fly aeroplanes, I thought, the next best thing to do would be to join an outfit whose job it was to shoot them down. I signed up for the Royal Regiment of Artillery and never looked back.

A year later, I found myself standing on the grassy runway, almost directly beneath the place where I had narrowly avoided a mid-air collision, my highly polished ceremonial boots firmly planted on the short grass. I was back at Middle Wallop, but this time I didn't even have time to glance up at the muggy, overcast sky. I was ready to add an overpowering stench of burnt cordite to the familiar and pleasant smell of freshly cut grass and aviation gasoline.

My duty that day was to command a detachment of gleaming ceremonial guns belonging to First Regiment, the Royal Horse Artillery, one of the most senior and highly respected units in the

British Army, and to ensure that the twenty-one-volley Royal Salute was delivered, for and on behalf of my old regiment, the Army Air Corps, in perfect unison. I couldn't take my eyes off the second hand on my precision watch as it ticked slowly around the clockface. Each of the six silver-and-green 55-pounders was numbered. It was my job to give the command for each gun to fire in the right sequence, exactly five seconds apart. I felt the huge pressure on my young and relatively inexperienced shoulders. Any slip-up would be obvious and highly embarrassing to the high-ranking officials escorting the Prince of Wales on the occasion of his presentation of Regimental Colours to the Army Air Corps, one of the youngest regiments in the Army.

I focused on my watch. I didn't have to turn and salute Prince Charles as he walked past my position because, when the guns are on parade, they take seniority and even the future king has to salute them. A bead of sweat dripped down my forehead, momentarily blurring my vision, but such was the booming rhythm of the guns, I found myself calling out in perfect time.

I forced myself to concentrate on the guns, counting each report and finally, to my huge relief, the last round was fired. Smoke drifted slowly across the runway. Now that the guns were silent, the busy little airfield seemed peaceful and unusually quiet. The only sound was the happy song of a skylark as it swooped for insects. All training had been halted, the aircraft grounded. I am proud of the regiment I joined after my failure as a pilot, and for just a fleeting moment, the smoke of the ceremonial guns blocked my sight of the helicopters lined up near the huge green hangars. However, this auspicious occasion did not block my awareness that in one week I would be taking up a posting to an old mill in beautiful, but very dangerous, South Armagh, on Northern Ireland's southern border.

After months of preparatory training, my regiment was about to deploy on a six-month, high-pressure tour to the heart of "Bandit Country". It had been hard working up to operational readiness. As well as the old ceremonial guns, the regiment was equipped with the very latest 155mm self-propelled howitzers, but for this operation, we were required to take on an infantry role. The boys were well drilled, exhausted and probably a bit bored with the specialist training; now they were ready to deploy. The final week before deployment, we were granted leave: a last chance to say goodbye to family and loved ones. *I'm so glad I'm not married with children*, I thought to myself.

CHAPTER 9

A Close Shave

I just loved being in the Army, whatever it had in store. I enjoyed the fact that it was a way of life; it owned me and in return it looked after me. The Army was so much more than my source of income; it was also my identity, my second family, my home. I was excited about our tour in Northern Ireland.

The day before deployment the commanding officer called the whole regiment together on the parade square. We were expecting a strong speech from our leader along the lines of: "Look about, lads; some of you may not return from this." Instead, he told us the tour was off. It was 1994: the Northern Ireland Peace Process was gathering momentum and fewer troops were needed. Politically, and for the people of Northern Ireland, this was excellent news, but for my unit cancellation of the tour was a big blow, a real anticlimax. There would be no medals, no operational pay and no opportunities for heroism that might cement a reputation for life.

Nevertheless, we were to remain on standby, at a high state of readiness for the next six months. Maintaining readiness meant we would have to continue to train hard without the rewarding prospect of a deployment. I threw myself back into the routines of training, and kept myself busy. Those six months passed quickly.

Unlike many others in the officers' mess (where I lived in some style with the other unmarried officers), I had no time for the distraction of a girlfriend. Instead, I volunteered for everything.

This included leading the Regimental Patrol Team on several long-range patrol competitions, which usually involved three days and two nights of non-stop high-speed "yomping" across very rugged terrain in the Brecon Beacons, being tested for various military skills along the way. For some reason, none of the other officers wanted to give up their weekends for such mad exploits, but I loved it and my small team of volunteers became the most highly trained men in the regiment.

It was during this time that I also had the privilege of commanding an honour guard for the Queen at the Bicentenary Celebration of the Royal Horse Artillery in the old Artillery Headquarters at Woolwich, London. I still have a picture of the Queen inspecting my troops, my Sword of Honour held straight in front of me. The picture hangs, as is the tradition, on the wall of my downstairs loo, with all my other military pictures. It was a happy time. But life in the Army was never entirely without risk.

In our Northern Ireland configuration, I was the battery operations officer. It was my job to plan all the anti-terrorist pre-emptive operations and also to co-ordinate any live response or follow-up in the event of an incident. As the second-in-command, if the battery commander (BC) was tied up or involved in an operation, it was my responsibility to step in for him and ensure the battery was still commanded.

During one of our many exercises, in which we trained for both urban and rural operations, I was busy planning a rural patrol. The intention was for me to plan the route and then for the BC to jump into one of the light, single-engine helicopters, called a Gazelle, to take a look at my proposed route from the air and confirm it. The Gazelles were very busy and it wasn't easy to secure the sortie, but I managed to book my BC onto a half-hour flight with my old friends from the Army Air Corps. However, although I had completed my plan and the BC's helicopter time slot was approaching, he was still tied up in a senior Orders Group and I had no idea when he would return.

By the time I heard the distinctive sound of the rotors approaching, the BC was still not back. I knew the helicopter would not wait, so I grabbed my weapon and my belt kit and ran to the helicopter landing site. The rotors continued to turn as I squatted close to the helicopter, waiting for the pilot's thumbs-up through the clear perspex of the bubble canopy. When it came, I ran forward to board the aircraft, making sure I kept my head low. I took my seat behind the two pilots. The aircraft commander, normally the senior pilot, doesn't usually fly the aircraft. He keeps a look out for lethal electricity cables and telephone wires while navigating the aircraft. I put on the huge green helmet and plugged in the intercom, so I could tell the pilots where I wanted them to fly me.

We'd been airborne for about fifteen minutes without incident. I'd seen most of the route, but I wanted to take a second look at something. As I gave that instruction, I felt a slight judder in the forward movement of the helicopter. I thought nothing of it. The pilots were talking to each other and I remember feeling slightly annoyed that they hadn't even acknowledged my instruction to turn and go back. I repeated my request and this time the aircraft commander calmly but authoritatively told me to "Wait out" – military-speak for "*Shut up!*"

The situation was more serious than I had realized. The commander's mayday signal told me that. *I don't want to die. I shouldn't even be here*, I thought to myself. The noise from the single-turbine engine reduced significantly as it shut down; all the time the pilots kept talking to each other and professionally went through what looked like well-rehearsed procedures. Before the incident we were flying quite fast and, by my estimate, at just a few hundred feet. Now the pilot arrested all forward momentum, but we were dropping rapidly. I was struck by the sudden quiet.

Helicopters have complex control surfaces and gearing. A major system failure to the main rotor or the smaller tail rotor can be catastrophic, but on the plus side, if the power is lost they can theoretically land by "auto-gyration". As the helicopter falls from the sky, the rotors will turn, generating at least some lift. The theory is that the rotors can then be "feathered", or turned to an angle that causes maximum lift, but will also cause the rotors to stop. This has to be done at precisely the right height. Too late, and the downward speed of the helicopter will not be halted in time; too early, and the helicopter will simply stop, stall and fall to the ground. I knew we were in the midst of an emergency. I knew we were falling fast, but I trusted the pilots completely. My life didn't flash before me, but I was very, very scared. All I could do was lean forward, put my head between my legs and pray.

We dropped. My tummy churned. *They've lost control, we're going to hit the ground*, I thought. At the last possible moment, I felt the thin blades above my head bite and our speed reduced. At the same time, I felt the power come back on and, just feet from the ground, we achieved a hover. I tried to say something, but both pilots completely blanked me.

After we landed and shut down, one of the pilots told me what had happened. He was as white as a sheet. It reminded me of the look on my instructor's face after my near miss. There must be something about me and aircraft that just is not right.

Both pilots were pretty certain that the slight judder I had felt was a possible shear in one of the rotors. Had the rotor come off, it would have meant certain catastrophe. Taking no chances, they had shut down the turbine in mid-flight. With three rotors still turning, at least they had a chance of landing safely. I felt an adrenaline rush for the whole two-hour walk back to Headquarters. I was elated, glad to be alive.

Gunner officers rarely serve consecutive tours in the same regiment, and my time had come to move on. There was only one regiment in the Royal Artillery I wanted to join, and it was with great excitement that I received my transfer papers instructing me, with typical Army politeness, to report to the Royal Citadel in my favourite county of Devon. But I wasn't going on holiday. I was finally going to get the chance to try and join an elite regiment and become a commando gunner. I would have to pass one of the most physically challenging military selection courses in the world. I could hardly wait.

CHAPTER 10

Fully Committed

It felt like Sandhurst on day one as I drove through the imposing gates of the Royal Citadel. The officers' mess overlooks Plymouth Sound. In summer and winter the views are quite stunning.

The Citadel's close proximity to the Barbican marina makes it a dream posting for "singelys" (Army slang for an unattached soldier/officer). The marina's pubs and restaurants attract nurses from the nearby Derriford hospital and students from the university. However, I had no thoughts of "running ashore" (a night out in Navy slang). I knew I had to pass the selection course before I could let my hair down.

Although I was a captain on my second tour, I knew I would have no respect from the soldiers until I passed the commando course and earned the right to wear the green beret. The Royal Marines Commandos are an elite fighting force with a great reputation for aggression with intelligence, but they rely on the Army to provide support in terms of engineers, artillery and logistics when required. The Royal Marines are part of the Royal Navy, not part of the Army, so, in order to ensure mutual respect, the Army insists that all units supporting the Marines pass the same selection tests as the Marines. Until I passed the course, I wouldn't really belong there. I was 100 per cent focused on getting to the next stage: Lympstone, the home of the Royal Marines.

Six weeks passed. We reached the end of March, but there was still no sign of spring. I had just survived three days of speed marching across Dartmoor and I had so many blisters on my feet, it was extremely painful to walk. This was the last day of the pre-course selection. If I passed, I had a weekend off and would report for the course at Lympstone on Monday. If not, I had to repeat the whole six-week experience.

Of the group of twenty who had started out, there was only a handful of us left. I had passed all the tests so far, but I still had to prove that I could scale the fifteen-metre rope in full kit. I'd managed it once before without kit, but I knew my technique was poor: I pulled myself up using the strength in my arms alone. I still had to prove I could do it the right way. The instructors knew I needed to use my legs, so they took me to a wet and muddy corner of the field near the ominously tall rope frame and there they made me do press-up after press-up, in full kit – slowly, to their own timing.

"Down," called the instructor I now hated. I dropped as low as I could without letting my chest touch the mud.

"Lower... Sir." I felt the weight of a size-ten boot pushing down on my back, until my biceps were burning. My arms began to shake uncontrollably.

"Up." At last I felt a second of relief as the screaming muscles in my arms locked out.

"Keep your bloody back straight, Larcombe... Sir."

Now all I wanted was to drop down again, but still he paused. *Maybe I won't make it to the top of the rope, but I will not give in*, I thought as my face sank in the stinking red mud.

After what seemed an eternity I was finally told to take my place in line. I was the last to go. I looked at the rope, which was now wet through and shiny smooth from the attempts of all the others to scale its full length. My arms felt so heavy I could hardly lift them; the weight of my equipment pulled me down as I waited in line, and the muzzle of my rifle dug painfully into my back. I remembered my failed attempt at flying training, how I had fallen at the last hurdle. I began to panic, just like I had when I tried to land. This time I prayed. I knew there was no way I could lift myself up the rope. But I prayed, just a simple prayer: "Your will, you do it."

"You're next, Captain Larcombe. Up you go."

And then something strange happened. I wasn't suddenly filled with super-human strength; I just felt an inner peace. Everything seemed to fade around me – the shouting of the staff, and the cheering from the others who had already made their ascent. It was just me and the rope. I had no strength in my arms, so for the first time, I looked down at my feet and wrapped the slick rope tightly around my wet, muddy boots. The rope held, so I pushed up from my knees. I didn't pull with my arms – I couldn't. Like a caterpillar, I locked the rope firmly between my feet and pushed. Again and again I repeated this movement and slowly I made progress. Then I looked up and, to my surprise, I was at the top! I had done it.

My completion of the pre-commando course had exhausted me. That night the lure of my bed and a few hours' sleep was stronger than any desire to celebrate. It hardly felt fair when I woke the following morning with symptoms resembling a hangover. Something dragged me from my deep, dreamless sleep. Slowly I opened one eye. I recognized my room. It was one of the smallest in the officers' mess. I was half-dressed and aching all over. I remembered trying to take my clothes off the night before, then giving up from exhaustion.

What *was* that annoying buzzing noise? Struggling into consciousness, I realized that my mobile phone was ringing incessantly from the desk near the door. Slowly, I lifted myself up. It was a Bank Holiday weekend and I had three days before the commando course started. I wanted to spend most of the weekend asleep, to recover from the lack of sleep while I had been yomping across Dartmoor. I also had to wash my kit, pack and eat. I had no intention of doing anything else. But someone really wanted to talk to me.

Very slowly, I sat up and tried to put some weight on my damaged, blistered feet, but quickly sat back down as I felt the tightness of the dry, red, raw skin begin to crack. I lay back, hoping whoever it was would go away, or maybe the battery would die before I did. But still the phone rang. Eventually I made it across the room, leaving a little trail of fresh blood on the carpet.

"Hello," I said groggily, making no effort to disguise my annoyance at being woken at 9 a.m. on a Saturday morning.

"It's me. Dunc. You still on for the weekend?" And then I remembered. Weeks before, I had agreed to play rugby in a tournament with my brother and some of our friends. The competition was due to be played a few miles along the coast from Plymouth in the beautiful sailing town of Salcombe. I could hardly stand, let alone run around on a rugby field, but Duncan would not take no for an answer.

I somehow made it through the weekend, probably numbing my pain with too many beers. But it was a fantastic weekend. Not only did we win the rugby, but I met Emma and Charlotte Stearn, beautiful and very mischievous twins. I sometimes wonder what would have happened if I had slept through the ringing of my phone that fateful morning. Having met Emma, the commando course seemed to fly by. There was little time for us to see each other, but I took every opportunity I could, dashing up to London on the occasional Friday evening and catching the Sunday overnight sleeper from Paddington back to Exeter, just making the 07.30 parade on Monday morning. At one point I injured my elbow just before one of our few leave weekends. The elbow became infected. I took the saline drip with me on the train to London, so determined was I to see Emma. It wasn't long before we were engaged.

The commando course was as tough as I had expected, but I worked my way through. As June approached, so did the final, toughest part of the whole course. I braced myself for my hardest challenge yet. The culmination of the course is the 30-miler – a gruelling endurance and speed test from one side of Dartmoor to the other in full kit plus weapon. It has to be completed in under six hours. This means you basically have to run the entire distance and under no circumstances can you afford to make a navigational error, not even a small one, because you just cannot make up the time. There is no flexibility. One minute over time is one minute too many.

I woke early enough to see a perfect sunrise above a barren moorland interspersed with small streams and ancient rocky outcrops. My adrenaline was pumping as the temperature began to rise. After coming this far, no one wanted to fail. But, because it was the last test, we were all carrying some form of injury. Before breakfast, we carefully taped up different parts of our aching bodies, took on fluids and made final checks of our kit. Of course, no one wanted to carry a single ounce more than they needed to, but there was also the fear that our kit might be weighed and found to be under the required amount. You don't get a second chance at the 30-miler. Failure today would mean starting the whole course again.

The 30-miler is completed in groups of five. We'd all heard the stories of groups getting lost in the fog that could descend at any time of the year, day or night. I had checked and re-checked my route. "Please Lord, don't let me get lost today. Let the sun shine, but don't let it get too hot."

For the first few hours, all went well, the cool morning temperatures and good visibility allowing us to hit our checkpoints right on time. But as the temperatures started to climb in the afternoon and fatigue started to bite, we knew that the dreaded Heartbreak Ridge still lay ahead of us.

Heartbreak Ridge is legendary on the commando course. The last obstacle standing between you and your right to wear the green beret, this hill, while not necessarily steep, seems to go on forever with ridge after energy-sapping ridge. Just as you think you have made it to the top, there is another crest and then another. As we ascended due south, the sun blazed constantly in our eyes and the temperature climbed as steadily as we did.

Heat exhaustion is a killer. It claims the lives of those who are so desperate to achieve, they don't listen as their bodies scream at them to slow down, cool down and take on water. We were well trained to recognize the symptoms of heat exhaustion in ourselves and in others around us. I started to grow concerned about one of my group, Chaz. His eyes were glazed and, unusually for the short Scotsman, he'd been pretty quiet for the last hour. We had made good time and I knew, just as all the others knew, that it was all downhill after The Ridge. It was time to stop and take on fluids, to cool down and take a breather.

A couple of the lads didn't want to stop; they felt good and they wanted to keep going. But we all knew we had to stay together. If the group split and we crossed the line individually, we might be failed, regardless of the time. Nor could we carry Chaz's kit. If we did, he would fail. Each person had to achieve the time with the weight. After a short stop, we pressed on. Then at last, there was relief as we finally crested the last ridge; enough relief to carry us down the hill and across the line. We were presented with our green berets there and then. There's no swanky parade and no family to see this private presentation, but it was one of the best moments of my Army career.

Life as a commando gunner was always exciting. For much of my time I was part of a Rapid Reaction Force, ready to deploy at short notice anywhere in the world. This also meant I had to complete an Arctic Warfare training course, a highlight of which was jumping naked into a hole cut through the ice of a frozen lake, then rolling in the snow to warm up. In stark contrast, I also had to attend the Jungle Warfare training school, where I made the mistake of bedding down on a giant ants' nest one night. I now know what it feels like to be eaten alive. I also narrowly escaped being struck by lightning while carrying a large radio with a tall antenna protruding from my pack. The tree six feet to my right snapped in half with the impact, and the crack was louder than any gun I have heard. I also had the thrill of refreshing my parachute training. I was hardly ever in the UK.

In the year Emma and I were due to be married, my unit was chosen to join a Commando Group, sailing from the UK to the Far East, conducting amphibious training at various points along the way. The culmination of the nine-month deployment and the purpose of the whole trip was to make sure a significant, fully trained fighting force was available just off the coast of Hong Kong during the formal handover to the Chinese, in case of any unrest that required military intervention.

After months of hard training we were ready. Our small taskforce moved into position, having been trailed by Chinese missile destroyers, with their launch tubes threateningly pointing directly at us. There was little we could do to show them we were not intimidated, as the ancient Royal Fleet Auxiliary ship (a sister ship to the *Sir Galahad* that was famously sunk during the Falklands War) only had a tiny space on which a helicopter could just land and where the men took their daily exercise. However, we improvised and showed the Chinese how battle-ready we were by conducting an unarmed combat demonstration and abseiling out of a helicopter. Then, just as we were about to take up our station just out of sight of the land, the worst happened. Our engines suffered complete mechanical failure, leaving us bobbing up and down on the South China Sea. Had we been needed, we would have been completely unable to respond. We had an immediate meeting on the officers' deck and decided not to tell the men. There might have been a mutiny!

Our engagement must have been quite hard on poor Emma. Having returned from Hong Kong, I spent the next six months back at Sandhurst attending the Junior Division of Staff College. The exams at the end of the course are quite tough and have a huge bearing on future promotion. Emma left me alone to study, while she took on the no-less-formidable task of planning our wedding day. The wedding reception was held at the Royal Citadel in Plymouth on one of the hottest days in 1997. It was unforgettable.

Duncan did a fantastic job as best man. In my regiment, it was traditional to stand on the dining-room table of the officers' mess when delivering any form of address over dinner. Not wishing to break with tradition, Duncan stood up, but didn't see the full pint of beer left alongside his carefully prepared notes. The pages were soaked and illegible, but Duncan spoke for forty minutes without them. His speech was so good that one of our guests laughed so much they fell off their chair and broke their wrist!

Emma and I moved into a lovely married quarter on a quiet estate in Plymouth. It was our first house and we wanted to make it a home, so we worked through the night unpacking all our things, including wedding presents. We unpacked the last box at dawn, leaving just enough time to pack suitcases for our honeymoon. We left that day. By a miracle I managed not to fall asleep while driving to the airport.

Two weeks later, upon our return home, we were welcomed by a set of posting orders on the doormat. My next posting had arrived early. We repacked all of our boxes, and ten days later unpacked them again in our new house in North Yorkshire. We had only been married a few weeks, and already we were in our second house. This was the second of the seven moves we would make in just five years. Fortunately, we were young, and Emma was a brilliant home-maker, able to put down roots almost overnight. But the uncertainty and lack of stability was unsettling her. She was five years younger than me. Only twenty-two, she still harboured dreams of an idyllic life. I feared her dreams might be hard to realize while the Army had first call on my time and perhaps, in retrospect, on my loyalty. Maybe I had a more nomadic outlook, because nothing seemed to deflect me from my absolute love for the military way of life. My career was being fast-tracked and I was enjoying the ride.

By Monday morning I was ready to report for duty to the commanding officer of my new regiment, the Lowland Gunners. I was a little nervous because already the CO wanted to discuss my performance at the Junior Division of Staff College. I left that meeting feeling on top of the world. I had achieved a staff pass, which meant I was eligible to attend Staff College itself, a must for officers aspiring to reach senior ranks and all the high-profile commands. He also promoted me to acting major. At the age of twenty-nine, this meant I was one of the youngest majors in the British Army. But probably best of all, the CO confided in me that the regiment was next in line to deploy to war-torn Bosnia in a peace-keeping role.

That evening, I broke the news of my promotion to Emma. It was somewhat harder to talk about the operational tour, which would mean six months away from home. We had only been married for three weeks, so I held back. Emma was delighted about the promotion, which meant more money. However, it also meant that we were entitled to a bigger home on a smarter part of "The Married Patch". The thought of moving into our third home in close to as many weeks filled me with dread. I could see nothing wrong with our current two-bedroom house, but Emma, undaunted, insisted on moving as soon as one of the four-bedroom quarters became available. Within two weeks we were in home number three!

The next six months flew by. As the operations officer, I had to ensure that the regiment had sufficient training and that all our equipment was packed and shipped over to Split on the Croatian Adriatic coast. On this tour we would be "in role", which meant we had to sharpen our gunnery skills. The regiment was equipped with the largest-calibre artillery in service, and our options in the UK for training were quite limited. This meant a large part of our pre-deployment training took place in the wide-open ranges of Canada.

Poor Emma. Not only did she have to prepare herself for her husband's extended absence on an operational tour to a nasty war zone, but even before deployment, I was hardly ever at home. Living in a lovely but remote part of the country where she had few friends was also difficult. All the other wives knew each other, but Emma was new, and younger than most of them. I should have seen the signs, but I was so wrapped up in making sure the deployment was planned properly, I guess I didn't give her the attention she needed. She must, at times, have wondered what she had done in marrying me.

CHAPTER 11

Dandelions and Daisies

"Boss, you need to call home."

The chief clerk looked quite concerned as I walked into the makeshift office we had set up as our Regimental Headquarters. It was the second week of a six-week training exercise in Canada. He left the room as I dialled the code for an outside line and then the international number for the UK, then the code for North Yorkshire. My hand was shaking slightly and I had to redial twice before I was connected. It rang out twice and I glanced at my watch. A quick calculation told me it was about 2 a.m. in the UK.

When Emma picked up the phone she broke down in tears and it was hard to understand what she was saying.

"What's up? What's the matter? What's happened?" I said, really worried now. "Are you hurt?"

"No, I'm fine, but you need to call your mum."

"It's Dad, isn't it? Has he had a heart attack, a car accident?" I asked.

"No, no, nothing like that, but please just call your mum." I could get nothing else out of her, so I dialled Mum's number in Kent.

"What's happened, Mum?" I asked as soon as she picked up the phone. There was a long pause before she finally answered. Her voice was a little shaky, but it was also full of resolve. The immense strength was still there, beneath the surface.

She said quite simply, "Your dad left today."

I had no idea what she meant. "You mean he's gone to a conference? For how long?" I wondered what all the fuss was about.

"Forever – he's left forever. There's someone else. He's left me… us – for someone else."

We spoke for a while. Afterwards, I went for a walk. It was cold. Heavy snowflakes twisted and whirled as they fell from nicotine-coloured clouds. Even though I was in shock, my mind still raced, looking for clues and trying to understand why this could have happened. I had never witnessed a single argument between my parents in all my life. Dad had stood by and supported us all through the years of Mum's illness. I'd last seen them during a leave weekend. My dad had been distant. I had thought, at the time, that it must be difficult being known primarily as "Jen Rees Larcombe's husband". Perhaps I could have guessed then that something wasn't right, but after thirty years of marriage, you assume your parents are indestructible.

After Mum's sudden healing, her diary had quickly filled with speaking engagements. Dad left his job in education to support her work. But that must have left him relegated to the sidelines. One day, I suppose, he must have formed a friendship that developed. I felt for Duncan and Richard, who still lived at home. I wondered how it would affect them.

As I trudged through the slush, I suddenly began questioning everything my dad had ever told me and all the advice he had ever given me. If he could go behind our backs and walk out on his family for someone else, then maybe everything he ever said was just a lie? In the years that followed I came to question the validity of many childhood experiences.

As I walked, a memory from long ago, of a conversation with Mum, reawakened in my mind. I was five or six, had just started school and my mum met me at the school gate. It was the summer term; I remember seeing bright-yellow dandelions and daisies in the thin strips of grass beside the pavement.

"I love you, Mummy," I said as I looked up at her face. She smiled and I remember feeling pleased that my words had made her happy, so I said, "I love you more than the whole world." But this time, her face became much more serious.

"I love you too, but one day I hope you'll love your wife more than me," she said.

"I'll never get married. I'm going to live at home forever and love you the best."

I will never forget her next words. "Justyn," she said, "the most important decision you ever make is to marry the right person."

As the Canadian snow changed to cold wet sleet, I looked at my life from the new perspective that today's news had given me. After all these years, would Mum now think she had married the wrong person? My thoughts turned to my own marriage. *What if I've married the wrong person?* I wondered. *What if Emma sometimes wonders the same?*

After walking for about an hour, I decided not to think too much about it. Although I worried about the devastation Mum must be feeling, I didn't have time to ponder how I felt about it, or the effect it might have on my brothers and sisters. I was about to deploy to a war-torn country: what could I possibly do about my parents' torn-apart lives? There was little enough I could do about the effects of my deployment on my own marriage. In my own typical way, I buried the hurt I felt at losing my dad. I probably also buried my concerns about me and Emma. I turned my mind back to the Army.

I don't think Mum has ever recovered from the loss of her friend and companion. I don't talk about it with her very often, but we have spoken of it recently. Each day for several years she expected to hear the door open and Dad to shout, "Hi, I'm home!" He never did. And then one day, Mum received the formal divorce letter from Dad's solicitor, and it finally hit home. Rather than slipping into depression, Mum typically channelled all the negative energy into something positive and trained as a bereavement counsellor. She now leads a team of people who are dedicated to helping those who have experienced loss, either through divorce or bereavement. Rather than wallowing in self-pity, she has helped hundreds of people. But I do know that if Dad walked through her door and asked her to take him back, she would open her arms wide and never once ask him why he hurt her.

When parents split, they stop being husband and wife, but they never stop being Mum and Dad, and I do think that it has a fundamental effect on the children, regardless of their age.

CHAPTER 12

All or Nothing

Bosnia in 1998 was not a nice place to be. The former Yugoslavia had been successfully held together by Tito, a Second World War anti-Nazi partisan hero. Although known by many as a benevolent dictator, his grip on the country had been as effective as a vice, holding together disparate parts of an extremely divided population with very deep-seated differences and a history of bloody conflict. After his death in 1980, the vice's hold loosened and it seemed inevitable that the region would once more descend into civil war. And so it did. By the early 1990s, Muslim Bosnians fought Orthodox Serbians and Catholic Croats, village fought village, and family fought family. Each element sought the total extermination of the other with "ethnic cleansing" on a horrific scale and huge rape camps where women of all ages were brought so they might be "cleansed" by bearing the children of the other side.

By the end of 1995 it is estimated that 100,000 had been killed (the figures cannot be verified, as few records were kept and mass graves were common), between 20,000 and 50,000 women had been raped and over 2.2 million people had been displaced, making it the most devastating European conflict since the end of the Second World War.

Just over two years after the ceasefire, tensions were still at boiling point, huge areas of the country were still heavily mined and the true horrific scale of the conflict was only just emerging. It was against this backdrop that my regiment, the Lowland Gunners, deployed as part of a multinational peacekeeping force. In the centre of an old metal factory on the outskirts of the Serbian town of Banja Luka, I lived in a tin hut that had once been a ship's storage container. In the summer, even the temperatures at night were unbearable and when the weather finally broke in September, sleeping in a metal box during a spectacular electric storm was out of the question.

The country was in a real mess. My role meant I was needed in headquarters, on call twenty-four hours a day, so when the opportunity arose to see some of the country, I jumped at it. Now I regret my enthusiasm and wish I'd stayed back in camp. The things I saw on my travels still haunt me to this day.

There was one particular village that, prior to the war, would probably have been quite similar to many villages across northern Europe. It was built on a gently sloping hill. At the top of the hill was a large primary school, surrounded on all sides by what would once have been smart brick houses. These houses were now piles of rubble.

We slowly weaved our way through the devastated village in our reinforced Land Rover. My driver was a thick-set sergeant, the kind you'd want next to you if it kicked off in the bar where you were drinking. He'd been here before and now, as he talked, he had tears in his eyes. The village had recently been the centre of a war crime investigation. It had been ethnically cleansed. Troops had moved into the village, rounded up the men and either shot them or taken them away to labour camps. The women were loaded onto cattle lorries and taken to rape camps. The gas cookers in each house had been turned on, but not lit, and large church candles had been placed in the upper floors. The windows and doors had then been closed. When the gas built up enough to reach the bare flames, it caused an explosion, flattening each home. One by one.

And the children...?

Sadly, it was quite obvious what had happened to them. In the playground, in a wall against which footballs would once have been kicked, a long line of bullet holes revealed where the children had been murdered. I wondered if they had died first or whether they had witnessed the death of their fathers and the deportation of their mothers. I still can't understand how humankind can be so ruthlessly cruel to other humans. The scariest thing of all was that this atrocity could well have been perpetrated by people living just a few miles away.

On the way back, after having my fill of destruction, I noticed a school bus that had veered off the road and into a ditch. It had obviously lain there several years and the undergrowth was now covering the underside, but the line of bullet holes along the entire length of the bus was still very clear.

I was upset by what I had seen. I never again volunteered for a trip outside the wire. Sometimes, it feels better to contain your experiences and your emotions. On this occasion, I tried to contain mine within the perimeter of the Army base.

However, an important part of my life existed beyond that fence, back home in England. Without a mobile signal, my communication with Emma was limited to letters and a weekly phone call with a military phone card. My calls were becoming more strained. I had little of interest to tell her. Most days in Bosnia were boringly repetitive for me, and if anything out of the ordinary happened, it was either quite nasty or just not possible for me to share over an open line. With nothing to say, I began to dread making the weekly call. It was clear Emma was not finding it easy on her own in a large house on a deserted Army base, but there was nothing I could do. There were wives' groups, but Emma felt excluded. Eventually, she moved back to her parents' house, which helped, but I was worrying about her as well as trying to keep my focus on a challenging operational tour. If I were to make mistakes and send a patrol along an uncleared route, people would die.

You might think that when a husband or a wife returns on leave from a six-month tour, the first few days are full of joy and happiness. The truth is, this can be a very difficult time. Those at home have learned to cope and don't necessarily like to give up their independence. The soldiers may have been through a lot and need some space to adjust. Although every soldier is entitled to two weeks' home leave during an operational tour, the timings are inflexible. So if your wife is pregnant, leave is planned around the due date. If the baby decides to be born during the last day of leave, that's tough luck – you still report in and fly back out so others can take their turn. It's quite possible that soldiers may be seeing their children for the first time on the day they arrive home.

On my first day back, I was elated. Rather than putting on a big party with friends, Emma was sensitive enough to realize a quiet home-cooked dinner for two was all I wanted. It's the simple things that we all take for granted that I missed. A double bed, a newspaper which has news stories that aren't a week old, and soft loo paper!

It was on the second day of my leave that I realized things were not all right. Over dinner at The Lobster (a quirky pub crammed full of junk and easily our favourite place to eat), Emma told me how difficult she found my being away. The British Army had just committed troops to Kosovo and I knew that there would be many operational tours ahead. We talked about many things, but it was really obvious that I had a choice to make. I had to choose between my Army career and my marriage. It was never phrased like that and Emma would never have been so direct, but I knew that our marriage would never last if I was away all the time. It was all or nothing.

We spent my two-week leave talking about little else. I had no idea what I would do outside the Army. It was so much more to me than a job; it really was a way of life. It was my identity and my future. I had a career plan that would take me up to the age of fifty-five and then give me a generous pension. It was well paid; we had a house, medical and dental provision, assistance with school fees if we had children. I played sport on Wednesday afternoons, rarely worked on Fridays after lunch and I got to see the world. Above all, it was something I felt I was quite good at.

But I also knew that if I was going to launch into another profession and start at the bottom of the pile, it would be better to do it now as I turned thirty. The next day, with many regrets, I signed my resignation papers. I felt as though I was turning my back on an old friend who had always been there for me and never let me down. I still dream I'm in the Army, leading my soldiers or trying to do the commando tests again. I miss it so much, but life in the services is tough on families, and operational tours are the hardest to cope with.

In some ways, my decision reminded me of when I gave up my swimming for Sasha. Six months after Bosnia, I handed back the uniform I had been so proud of and walked out of the camp gate to where Emma was waiting for me. The guard at the gate did not salute me as I passed. I was no longer a major, I was just a Mr. Had I done the right thing? I had experienced the thrill of managing hundreds of people in a high-pressure, operational environment; I had had a certain amount of status, a reputation and a career for life, if I wanted it. I was turning my back on a way of life I loved, in exchange for a desk job with no responsibility, half the wage and nowhere yet to live. I was about to become a very junior insurance clerk in a small town in Hertfordshire.

PART 3

Just Business

There's a way of life that looks harmless enough;
look again — it leads straight to hell.
Sure, those people appear to be having a good time,
but all that laughter will end in heartbreak.

PROVERBS 14:12–13, THE MESSAGE

CHAPTER 13

The Bottom of the Pile

Emma didn't need a test to tell her she was pregnant. She already knew; the result just gave us both something to celebrate. I was delighted. We had exchanged our four-bedroom house for the basement room at Emma's parents' until we found a home of our own. After all our moves, Emma felt she really wanted to build a nest close to her roots, and we soon found a little cottage in Worcestershire. We used all my savings for the deposit, and almost all my salary would go on the mortgage. For me, this decision meant at least a three-hour drive between home and work; a drive which took in five different motorways. Doing this twice a day was out of the question. Besides, we calculated it would be cheaper for me to live in a flat during the week than to pay for so much petrol. So I left the house just after 4.30 a.m. each Monday morning and returned on Friday night. A bedsit was all I could afford.

In the office late one afternoon, the screen on the integrated telephone unit flashed a familiar number. My team leader wasn't happy. "Oh crap," she sighed, "it's Mrs Robson again. I just can't face her at five to five. She'll be on the line for at least half an hour. Justyn, you talk to her." She passed me the headphones with the little microphone built in.

"Sure," I smiled back, quite happy to be given the responsibility of talking to a real client. I was fed up with hour after hour of role play with the young chap from the training team. It's difficult to keep interested in your fourth session of "The Three Steps to

Good Communication". Now I had a real client and I didn't care if the office was closing at five. With only my bedsit to return to, I would quite happily talk to Mrs Robson for half an hour, although I did hope she wasn't expecting too much of a technical answer.

By the time the call ended (the display screen told me I had been "live" for exactly twenty-nine minutes and thirty-three seconds), the office was empty. Although this was only my third week, I had already grown to love the calm and quiet of an empty office in contrast to the chaos between 9 a.m. and 5 p.m. This was the best time to study, and it had become something of a routine for me to stay late since I had signed up for my Insurance Associateship exams. The only day I left the office at the same time as everybody else was Friday, when I drove eagerly back home to the Midlands, and to Emma.

Besides, it was impossible to study in my tiny bedsit, where a small and flimsy fold-down table was attached to the grease-smudged wall. It was directly above a large, noisy family, making the task of concentrating on "The Measurement of Financial Risk" even more difficult than it would otherwise have been. So I stayed at my desk. Although no one else on my floor worked after five, I wasn't the only one in the building to work late. The Managing Director always popped his head in at 8 p.m. on his way home and sometimes came over for a chat. He was interested to hear about my life in the Army and encouraged me to keep studying. He had passed his exams twenty years before, and they had certainly helped him climb the ladder. If I sat two exam subjects every six months, I could be qualified in two and a half years. Until I qualified, I didn't mind being told what to do by people ten years younger than me. It was all part of the experience, and I was eager to learn from anyone. Besides, I really liked the others in the office. And they knew about insurance, whereas I knew nothing at all. But I did know about people and I did know how to communicate with old Mrs Robson; she lived alone and just wanted to chat to someone. Perhaps she and I had something in common.

The Bottom of the Pile

The truth is, I dreaded going back to my bedsit. It was freezing cold and the single-bar electric heater drank my pound coins. Most nights, I delayed my departure from the office until the cleaners were locking up and I had to leave. I would gather my papers and put the thick study text into my briefcase, button my coat against the cold and, leaving the bright lights of the office, I would head back to my shabby bedsit. On a good night, my neighbours would have finished drinking their rum punches and gone to bed by the time I turned the key in my door. It wasn't much fun trying to sleep when they were still up. Bad though the evenings were, it was the mornings I dreaded most. I had to wait my turn to use a shared shower at the end of the freezing corridor. The rusty shower-head dribbled lukewarm water and the meter greedily swallowed my 20p coins.

Although the bedsit was really, really grotty, my Army experiences had taught me to handle discomfort. By far the worst thing was being away from our newly arrived son Harry. His little face lit up every time I got back on Friday nights. I could put up with the living conditions, but I really missed being a proper dad, being at home as he grew up. Perhaps the emptiness I felt during the week provided the motivation to work as hard as I could. I suppose I knew I wouldn't be there forever, and hard work might speed things up. I had a plan. It just meant a lot of hard work.

I actually quite enjoyed insurance. I enjoyed the buzz of the office, the banter and the demanding clients. I had no hesitation in asking questions and went out of my way to befriend the key characters, in the hope that they would explain how the office functioned. I was soon moved to the VIP team, which meant working with the more valuable clients; this was probably because I was confident on the phones, certainly not because I knew anything about insurance. My willingness to take the difficult calls seemed to make me quite popular among my fellow workers, all of whom were at least five years younger than me. I think I was seen as a bit of a novelty. Everyone in the office had a nickname and it wasn't long before I had mine. It was inevitable.

"Morning, Major! Do you want to join our syndicate?" It was 8.30 in the morning and just a few of the team leaders were starting to arrive. I noticed copies of *The Sun* spread on top of heaps of client files. The office joker, Adrian from the Motor Department, was a likeable chap who would have been just as at home selling cars as he was advising the wealthy on how to insure them.

"What is it?" I asked, glancing down at the page of celebrities' names he'd been staring at. I recognized a few famous names. One or two had bold red lines drawn through them.

"It's our celebrity funeral sweepstake. You put twen'y quid in the pot and choose someone famous who you think'll pop their clogs next. If they do, you take all the money. You can do three names for fifty. Easy. Dan's just walked off with fifty quid because that John Thaw died last week."

I had been a bit sad when John Thaw died. *Inspector Morse* had been compulsory family viewing in the late 1980s and the 1990s. There was always a competition between my brothers and sisters to correctly guess the identity of the murderer. Sarah was the best at it. I never guessed right; I changed my mind too often.

I gave Adrian some excuse about not having any cash on me. The truth was I didn't have any cash in the bank either. I was living on tins of soup in the bedsit. The days of fine dining in the mess were a thing of the past. Now I ate from plastic rather than silver, and I certainly wasn't going to squander any precious pennies on a sweepstake.

As the weeks wore on I realized that the syndicate was the social hub of the office and Adrian was the controller. As well as people dying, the syndicate betted on every Premiership football match and many other sporting events. Their methods seemed quite sophisticated, but because it always involved cash up front, I avoided it.

One afternoon, I was chatting to Adrian. He told me he was going to Lloyds of London the following day and asked if I wanted to come along. I jumped at the opportunity and pestered my team

Age one with my elder sister Sarah in December 1969. I may look harmless, but I was a very difficult child.

My paternal grandfather, Sydney Larcome, taken during the Second World War when he worked for Royal Air Force Intelligence. He was never a warm grandparent, but I loved him all the same.

My grandmother, Otty, with my mother, and The Boss with my Uncle Justyn. Behind them is the first Hildenborough Hall, where my mother grew up.

This picture was taken in 1986 after winning a Southern Counties swimming club competition (I am at the top left). It is still displayed in the club's trophy cabinet at the swimming pool where I now train. It provided part of the inspiration for my solo Channel attempt.

The 1st XV rugby squad at the Judd School in Tonbridge, Kent, 1959. My dad is standing in the centre of the second row.

Officers of A Battery, The Chestnut Troop, 1st Regiment, Royal Horse Artillery, one of the most senior units in the British Army, taken in 1994.

A proud Para, 1989. I had just completed "P Company" – a tough military test that must be passed before being allowed to undertake military parachute training. I have two black eyes from "milling", a form of all-out boxing designed to test aggression.

My first house after I left the Army in 2001.

The Larcombe brothers in 2006. Richard is on the left and Duncan on the right.

On the beach in Devon with Harry, 2005. I was a weekend Daddy, but every weekend was packed full of fun and ice cream!

Dad and me in Kefalonia. This was taken on holiday in 2006 just after I resigned from my job to take up a new role closer to Emma. Dad moved to the Greek island with Val, his new wife.

In Val d'Isére on Emma's birthday in 2006. I had just proposed on the top of a mountain.

The day I married Emma, May 2007, was the happiest day of my life. The rings we had just presented each other I later sold to fund my habit.

We had a special uniform made for Harry, who was seven on our wedding day. He loved the Sword of Honour and enjoyed playing the role of "protector of the married couple".

A family holiday in 2010. Nothing distracted me from my online habit. I was probably checking a score, having made an excuse to check "work emails".

Christmas 2012, a really hard time. The first Christmas after our separation. At least Oscar enjoyed the food!

With a circulation of more than five million, going public in the *Daily Mail* in August 2013 was not an easy decision and caused a lot of hurt at first. It also helped a lot of people realise they too needed help.

Happy times at our favourite café, Captain Morgan's, in Salcombe, 2011. Harry on the left and a young Matthew in the middle. Oscar and Matty adore their big brother Harry.

leader so much that day, she finally let me go. It was an amazing experience. Lloyds is a huge modern building in the City and the global centre of insurance. The energy in the huge hall was palpable as smartly suited brokers and underwriters purposefully hurried past me, mobile phones stuck to their ears. We had lunch in one of the busy bars near Leadenhall Market. I knew right then that this was where I wanted to work. The very next day I asked my team leader how I could apply for a transfer to the London office.

"It's much too early, Justyn. You've only been in the company five minutes. They all do commercial insurance in the City, and what do you know about that?"

I tried to hide my disappointment. As I walked back to the bedsit, I felt myself agreeing with my team leader: I really knew very little about insurance, let alone commercial insurance. But my mind was buzzing, and that night I couldn't sleep. When morning came I had reached a decision. If my company didn't think I could work in London, I would find a company that did. By the time my team leader arrived and sat down at her desk, I had already made an appointment with a recruitment agent in the City.

Three months later, on 4 February 2003 (my thirty-fourth birthday), I walked up the imposing steps of my new office near Tower Hill. It wasn't even 8 a.m., but the office was in full swing. This was more like it. My new boss had taken a chance on me, so I had a lot to prove.

I worked hard from the outset, determined to make an early positive impression. Aware that I had to catch up with my work colleagues, I worked harder. Without any distractions at home, I could throw myself into the job. I made sure I was in early, working the phones, making appointments with prospective new clients, staying on after work with the other sales guys to share a beer and listen to how they achieved their success. The basic salary was still less than my Army wage, but there were opportunities for commissions and bonuses if I did well, and it wasn't long before I made my first sale. And then I made some more.

Only six weeks after I started, I was summoned to the Managing Director's office. Surely it could mean only one thing: I was going to get a roasting. He never, ever gave direct praise. I knocked at the door with trepidation. My hand was shaking as I turned the handle.

"I want you to come with me and visit a potential client. We're catching a train to Bristol on the hour, so pack your bags." There was no time for debate.

To be invited out to a first meeting with one of the MD's own prospects was a big step up. On the train journey to the West Country, we had more time to talk and I was surprised to hear that my sales figures had already been noticed on "the upper floors". This was the ultimate compliment. I loved the new challenge, and it seemed I was surprising everyone, not just myself.

When we finally got back to the office later that night, I had learned a huge amount. I couldn't wait to put into practice all I had picked up from my boss during the day.

But as my career took flight in London, my personal life was careering in quite a different direction.

CHAPTER 14

Break-up

I had been overjoyed to move out of my bedsit and start work in London. At first, I considered living at home with Emma and Harry, but Emma and I agreed that I should stay closer to work. So, during the week I stayed at Mum's, which meant that we could save as much money as possible. Our plan was to earn and save enough to buy a property closer to the office. So, when I made my first sale, it really was something to celebrate. Emma came down to join me for a London night out. We stayed with her twin sister's boyfriend at his flat in Chelsea. It was a great night, but as it grew late I felt exhausted. Thinking about work the next day, I left them all dancing in a club and made my way back to the flat and to bed. I often wonder what would have happened had I stayed out later. Or rather, what wouldn't have happened.

The following week, I managed to secure a meeting with a big manufacturing company in the Midlands. I arranged the meeting for a Friday, which meant I could go home on Thursday night: a rare treat. I thought I would surprise Emma and stopped on the way back from the station to buy the ingredients to cook her favourite meal.

I am certain that I was so tied up in my job that I was failing her as a husband. I had certainly failed to see the signs: her calls for attention, the secrecy with her mobile phone. After the meal, we stayed up chatting until quite late. I probably spoke too much about work. It was after midnight when we eventually went to bed.

Emma was in the bathroom when her phone rang. Surprised, I reached over to her bedside table. Before I could pick up the phone, Emma came rushing into the room and swept the phone away. But not before I had time to read the display. I recognized the name. It was a friend of her twin sister, one of the guys we had been celebrating with when I left the party.

I guess most couples would have sat down and talked it through. But all the time we had spent apart during our marriage had probably taken its toll. I think my pride was hurt and I put up a barrier that prevented painful discussions that would have helped. The look of sheer guilt on her face told me everything I needed to know. I packed my bag and left. That was the last time we spent together. I booked a counselling session for us, but in the end, I attended on my own and spent most of the hour feeling sorry for myself. We never really talked about things and the divorce went through very quickly.

I really don't blame Emma. She was very young when she fell for me as a dashing young officer. Now I was just an insurance salesman, and mostly absent. It really shouldn't have come as any surprise to me when she found the attention and friendship that she so rightly craved and deserved outside our marriage. I gave Emma the house in Worcester. She got married again quite quickly and we easily and amicably reached agreement on access for Harry. Emma and I are now best friends. She is a brilliant mother to our son. Although I grieved the loss of my son in my everyday life, I found strength and solace in the faith I had always held – my belief that everything happens for a reason, that there is hope in the God who created us.

In the months following my break-up with Emma, I missed Harry very badly. From the start, I saw him at least every other weekend, driving the six-hour round trip to collect him on Fridays and the same again to drop him off on Sundays. Every pick-up on Friday was the most wonderful experience, with all the excitement and anticipation of our weekend ahead. In contrast, every drop-off was agony. Before leaving to drive Harry home, I always made sure I tided everything away, because any evidence or reminder of our games, the books we had read or the films we had watched together, would cause me huge pain if I found them on my return. Often, driving home with the empty seat beside me, I would have to pull over, racked with grief.

Although I cultivated a thicker skin, I think I stored up all the emotion somewhere. I don't think I realized at the time just how much I was grieving the loss of my son, who was quickly growing up and who would now get older without me in the family home. I would forever be his father, but we were both going to have to get used to my role as a weekend dad. My heart was broken. I still grieve the fact that I haven't been able to be a constant presence for him.

But that's not all I grieve for. One of Harry's favourite games when he was little was playing with my sword. "One day, you will own it," I told him. I remember the pride in his little face. At such times, you never think that you might someday crush your child's dreams. Who could believe that of their future self?

CHAPTER 15

Lucky Breaks

With an empty house and more time to myself, I threw myself into my job with more passion than ever before. My last exams were looming. All my waking hours were dedicated to closing sales and revising for the final exams. The exams, and then the results, duly arrived. I had achieved a distinction in all six subjects, including the highest mark in the country for one of my papers, which meant a prize from the examination board as well as one from my company. When my boss called me in to congratulate me, I felt light-headed and happy for the first time since the breakdown of my marriage. The future looked bright again.

One hot Friday evening in mid August, I was working late again in the office, when my phone rang.

"Hi, Justyn, it's the Chairman here. Can you spare us a minute, please?"

I climbed up the stairs to his office, wondering what lay ahead.

Our company was the third largest insurance broker in the world. Five years previously, they had closed their private client business, retaining only a small pool of key clients and making well over a hundred people redundant. They had recently decided to re-launch this side of their business and I had volunteered to provide advice and insight into how our major competitor, the company I had previously worked for, operated in this exclusive and highly specialized field. My helpfulness had been noted. This hot Friday evening, the Chairman offered me a glass of Scotch and the role of Managing Director. With those few sips, and the brief formality of an interview process, I became one of the youngest Managing Directors of a division of one of the largest insurance broking companies in the world.

Realizing that my company had taken another chance on me, I relished the opportunity. More than ever I launched myself into the task. Life became a whirlwind. The division grew quickly and after a year we doubled our revenue. With my significant pay rise and early success, I soon had enough to afford the deposit on a cottage in Suffolk, close to the office where most of my staff would be located. I began to put down some roots and started to play rugby again for the local team.

Work was great. In my previous roles, I had built up many contacts who proved valuable to my newly formed and very effective team. We got some early, high-profile big wins and some high-profile clients. For these people, business was usually done through their advisers. The relationship with my most prominent client was conducted through an accountant who loved to play golf. Many of our discussions took place on the greens and fairways of the exclusive Wentworth Golf Club. Within our company, one department head approached me to ask for an introduction to this client. He wanted to offer the client the chance to insure his football team against winning the Champions League. The team had just reached the semi-finals. I wanted to know why they needed to insure *against* winning and said as much. The look I got in return made it very clear how stupid I was being.

"If they win, they'll have to pay the manager and all the players a win bonus of many millions of pounds. We can insure them at Lloyds, so if they win, the insurer pays out instead of the club."

"OK," I said, trying to sound knowledgeable. "How much would the premium be?"

"We'd have to work out exactly what the payout would be, but I reckon the premium would be close to 8 million plus insurance premium tax."

I tried not to choke on my wine. The introductory fee alone would mean I'd hit my annual target three months early. The next day I called my golf buddy at his office and made the proposal. He didn't seem fazed by the cost and promised to give it some thought. That afternoon he called me back.

"Hi, Justyn. I just wanted to thank you for making me aware of a potential exposure. We really liked the idea. So I sent someone down to William Hill. We backed the club. If they win, we get a payout that covers our exposure. Our stake was 8 million, but we don't have any insurance tax to pay."

I told him, through gritted teeth, how glad I was to have helped. And swore very loudly when I put the phone down. Never before had I considered any similarity between gambling and insurance. I didn't have long to dwell on such thoughts, nor on my lost opportunity. I was preparing a sales presentation for the entire insurance portfolio of the Royal Household. We didn't win that one either, but the process was fascinating, allowing me unprecedented access to the different Royal properties.

In spite of the setbacks, there were many gains. One Monday morning, as I parked my new car in my reserved space, and as golden rays of sunlight began to spill over the horizon, it suddenly dawned on me that I'd really achieved something. The day held promise and I couldn't wait to get to my desk. There were deals to be done, and money to be made.

Everything was happening for me so quickly, I hardly even had a chance to catch my breath. Flying over the Atlantic one day, heading for a meeting with the board of the investment bank Goldman Sachs on Wall Street, I reclined in my comfortable business-class seat and allowed myself time for reflection. What a year it had been. Was it just luck? On the one hand, I reflected, it could be no coincidence that the times in my life where I had experienced the most success were the times when I had relied on my faith. But now, at more than 30,000 feet above the Atlantic, I wondered whether faith had really been the key factor. Surely my abilities had played a part too. I felt pride in my own achievement. I enjoyed it when the financial press asked me to comment on a particular aspect of the insurance market; I liked being at the top table at insurance events and I liked being invited to socialize with other senior managers. This feeling of pride in my own ability has been one of the most destructive and debilitating forces in my life, but I didn't recognize it at the time and wouldn't until several years later.

By now I was receiving regular invitations to insurance industry events. Some I accepted, some I declined. One morning, I received one such invitation from one of the largest insurers I placed my clients' business with. This one, to a five-day conference with industry leaders, stood out from others. Not only would it offer an excellent opportunity to establish ties with key people, but it was in Las Vegas – expenses paid. It was an exciting prospect, but I decided that work was too hectic, and declined. Besides, what interest would I have in the epicentre of the gambling world? Similarly, I had an annual VIP pass to the Cheltenham races, but I never saw much of the racing – I was mostly networking in the bar. After all, I couldn't put a bet on my expenses, so why bother? Days out at races or big sporting events were common and often a tipster would be invited to our box to impart their knowledge. I just wasn't interested, though. I couldn't see the point.

One day I received an invitation to a breakfast at the Tate Modern art gallery in London with one of the leading insurers of fine art. I will never forget the speech I heard on that day, which for me captured the very nature of the world of insurance. His voice was low and wonderfully well rounded, inviting complete trust and attention from the hundreds of people in the room.

"Insurance is a gamble. I bet my clients they won't have a loss. Every year, they bet me they will, and they pay their stakes up front. Mostly I win. Which is why I'm a very rich man."

CHAPTER 16

New Beginnings

I loved my little cottage in Suffolk. I tended the garden, grew vegetables, took walks by the sea and read by the big open fire. Although it was a lonely place, I had no desire at all to share it with anyone, and I had no desire to be hurt again. A bachelor's life was appealing: I didn't need anyone, and if I didn't need them, they couldn't let me down. In short, I was content. And then spring came: a time of thaw and of new beginnings.

I was feeling happy as I drove to an executive management course at a country house hotel in the market town of Ashbourne in Derbyshire one blustery March morning. The proximity of Ashbourne to Worcester, where Harry lived, meant that after the course, on Friday evening, I would be able to pick him up straight from school and we would have more time together.

As I drove, I noticed the signs of spring all around. The last of the snowdrops were clustered beneath thickly budding trees. Seeing the clumps of daffodil shoots in the grassy verge, I reflected that it wouldn't be long before they were all flowering, adding vibrant colour to the hawthorn hedgerows which were already flicked with white blossom. I shared nature's energy and excitement. The course, with delegates from major companies such as Rolls Royce, Tesco and the BBC, promised opportunities to learn more about the world of business, and to meet interesting people.

I turned into the hotel's neat driveway and saw ahead of me a smart but quite imposing Victorian country house hotel. I later learned that the owners, Dorothy and David Spencer, had bought the neglected property twenty-five years before from an established family who had fallen on hard times. They poured their life into the business, turning it into a successful and highly sought-after hotel. While it made quite an impression on me, I had no idea of the part that hotel was to play in my future. I sometimes wonder what impression I made upon Mrs Spencer as I checked in. The first of the fifteen or so young executives to arrive, I had a badly bruised thigh from weekend rugby, and I could hardly lift my own bag as I followed her to the room I had been allocated.

After an hour or so, I wandered down to reception, thinking I might ask for some ice for the bruising. I am not sure if I really believed in love at first sight before that day, but I certainly do now. Mrs Spencer was sitting at the reception desk when I made my request for ice. She introduced me to her daughter, Emma, who was busy photocopying menus. Emma suggested we might go to the bar where there was an ice bucket. Mrs Spencer's daughter was strikingly beautiful and I was instantly taken by her stunning smile and clear blue eyes. I think I may have managed a thank you, and probably some stupid comment about Emma being my favourite name.

I don't remember any of the business management theory over the next three days. What I do remember is trying to work out different strategies for accidentally bumping into Emma, or engaging her in conversation. It must have been quite obvious to my fellow executives that I was completely smitten, because one of them, a kindly girl from the BBC, decided to take matters into her own hands and, much to my horror, went to have a quiet chat, girl to girl. As if by magic, the bar cleared and Emma and I were left alone to talk. I think I must have asked her if she would like to have a coffee sometime and it was then that I discovered she was dating a six-foot-ten-inch South African. But I must have been persistent, because the following weekend I found myself back in Ashbourne.

We met at the church. It was a beautiful spring day. The daffodils had now burst into flower, creating a carpet of gold in the churchyard. I know it sounds too cheesy to be true, but the birds *were* singing very loudly. Over coffee we discovered we shared an interest in gardening and architecture, as well as skiing, but all too soon it was time for her to get back to the hotel. We'd been together for half an hour and I had a three-hour journey back, but it was long enough for me to realize that I didn't want to be a bachelor any more.

The next year was hugely successful for me at work, but complete agony emotionally. Four months after I first met Emma, if I had had any doubts before, I knew for sure that I had fallen in love with her, on a day that will be forever remembered as one of the gravest days in the recent history of London.

On 7 July 2004, I found myself on the London Underground. My tube had just passed through Aldgate station when there was a brief power cut. I carried on my journey towards the West End without giving it much thought. I was annoyed that the tube was halted two stations before my stop and we all had to get off. There were apologies for widespread power disruptions and I can remember having to walk up a stationary escalator to the level of the street.

Blinking against the glare of a midsummer sun, I tried to get my bearings. I calculated it was only a ten-minute walk to my client's office. He was a wealthy Middle Eastern prince, one of our biggest clients. I couldn't risk being late, so I set off at military pace. As I marched along, I became aware of the noise of sirens. Not just one or even two, but many sirens coming from several different directions.

When I arrived, I found a number of well-suited business types, as well as several security staff, all gathered together around a big TV screen. I watched with mounting disbelief as the story unfolded. Details were quite slow at first, but it was clear that there had been a number of coordinated bombings against London's transport system at the very height of rush hour; buses had been targeted as well as a tube train just outside Aldgate station. Only later did I realize that, by a margin of about two minutes, I had missed being on the train that was partly destroyed by a suicide bomber.

All I could think of was Emma. I knew that over the weekend she'd been to see her boyfriend, who lived in London. I also knew that she normally travelled back on Monday mornings, taking the Underground back to King's Cross station and then catching the train back to Derby. I was glued to the TV as reports came in that the concourse at King's Cross had been targeted, and there were multiple casualties. I searched my pockets for my mobile, but when I found it, there was no signal; the network was swamped with people making urgent calls to their loved ones. It was clear that many people had been killed or injured.

When the receptionist called me upstairs into the office, I tore myself from the screen. Somehow I made it through the meeting, but all I could think of was reaching Emma. As I walked back from the West End towards the City, I prayed she would be somewhere safe. All around me was the sound of wailing sirens and the streets of central London were eerily deserted. That was when I knew for sure I was in love with her and I made a promise to myself that I would wait as long as it took for her to realize she felt the same about me. She sent me a text message the following day. I still remember all the words.

After eight long months that felt more like eight years to me, Emma ended her relationship with her boyfriend. The following month, on her thirty-first birthday, on the top of a mountain above the ski resort of Val d'Isere, she agreed to marry me. As I skied down the mountain that day, I was quite certain that there was no happier human being than me on the planet. I had found someone to share a life with, a companion and a friend. Emma was and will always be the only person ever to have truly known me. All I wanted was to look after her, to make her dreams come true and be loyal and loving until the day I died.

I was engaged to the girl of my dreams, but I lived and worked almost 200 miles from her home. This wasn't ideal. As Emma was committed to the family's hotel in Ashbourne, and as Harry was living just south of Birmingham with his mum and new stepfather, I was keen to find work in the Midlands rather than London. With such a move, I could be close to the people I loved.

I knew that the Managing Director of our Birmingham office had been promoted and the company was looking for a successor. Birmingham was the company's biggest office outside London, with a multi-million-pound budget. I boldly asked to be considered for the role. Two tense days later, I received the call I so desperately wanted from my immediate line manager.

"It has caused us a bit of grief, Justyn," he explained. "You've done really well with the division and there isn't an obvious successor, but we realize you need to move on and we don't want to lose you, so the Birmingham job is yours." Relieved and elated, I felt like leaping with joy, but a disappointment followed. "The post will not be vacant until December." It was only April.

I took the escalator up through the centre of the huge glass building, heading for the solitude of the roof garden, a huge strip of manicured turf. I needed to think. I was grateful for the opportunity, but in my mind I had made the decision to move on, and eight months seemed a long time to wait. Perhaps I could do better.

My secretary often fielded calls from recruiters, some speculative, some more specific and therefore more interesting than others. Unless I was really busy, I usually gave the agents time to explain who they were and where they were calling from, but up until that time I had always thanked them and explained I was happy in my job. Sometimes I gave them a name of someone else I thought might be suitable.

By coincidence, I had two calls the following week, both of them for national roles based in the Midlands, close to Harry and close to Emma. Both roles were available now. Rather than thanking them and putting the phone down, I found myself thinking about the jobs: what it would be like to be near the people I loved rather than having to do a six-hour drive every time I wanted to see them;

what the prospects were, the salary and benefits packages. I began to speculate, to daydream, and inevitably I agreed to interviews. I was offered both jobs. Both beat my current salary.

When I called Emma to ask her opinion, she suggested that I might try to speak to people who worked within the companies. It was great advice and after we said goodnight I tried to think of anyone I knew who might have a useful connection. The insurance broking industry is quite small; it's all about reputation and I was sure I would know someone.

The next morning was beautiful. There was little traffic on the roads as I drove to work. I felt alive, at the top of my career; I was in demand and it felt good. The sound of my new Porsche's engine thrilled me. My open roof allowed me to feel the wind on my face and smell the salty sea air, lending me great clarity of thought. I suddenly remembered that I had quite recently met someone who had worked at both the companies, but who was now working for a smaller, independent broker. I had his card in my desk. Long before anyone else had arrived at the office, I was up on the garden roof with my phone. My contact and I spent forty minutes talking about the merits and drawbacks of each organization, and then he paused.

"You know what the best thing you could do right now is, though, don't you?" he said.

"What's that?"

"Come and meet our chief exec. He's unbelievably charismatic. You could come and run our private client division, take a share of the company. We're talking big money, life-changing money. As a director you could be one of the shareholders."

This changed my game plan. I worked for a global company; I wasn't sure I would fit in at a small privately owned company. I also wanted to move on from the niche where I had made my name; I wanted to branch out of my specialist area. Nevertheless, I agreed to meet the chief exec a few days later. He was indeed charismatic, with exciting plans for the company. It was clear that his team loved him and shared his vision. We talked about the role and a package, which was more than I could have imagined. I voiced some reservations; the job was mostly in London. This wasn't what I had been looking for, but he offered me a generous resettlement package. I mentioned that in my current role I was on track for a big bonus, which I would have to forgo if I left; he offered a generous signing-on fee. Every time I raised a concern it was met with an offer I found hard to refuse.

After I had signed the contract, I felt elated. When I resigned from the job I had I came under pressure not to leave, but my boss realized my mind was made up, so they sent me home for a few months' gardening leave. I immediately booked a villa in Corfu and had a week in the sun to contemplate my good fortune. As I lay by the pool in my private villa, sipping a cold beer, I realized it had only been four years since I had been living in a bedsit, trying to make ends meet. Since then, I had made a name for myself in the competitive world of financial services. My salary had almost quadrupled; I had a lovely fiancée, my own house and two cars. I briefly thought about the officers I had served with in the Army, several of whom would now be serving in difficult operational conditions in Iraq or Afghanistan. Then I finished my beer. There were plenty more in the cooler.

CHAPTER 17

The Best Day of My Life

It felt as though every day of my life had led to this day. It was perfect. The church in Ashbourne was packed with all our friends and family. I was smiling so much my face hurt. My best man and closest friend Alex stood with me at the front of the church while we waited for Emma to arrive. I shifted nervously from one foot to the other, and pulled at the stiff collar of my dress shirt. The bells rang out their melody, clearly audible above the chatter of excited conversation.

The calm presence of Alex next to me was reassuring. A tall rock of a Welshman, he smiled as if to say, "She'll be here." Suddenly a hush descended and I turned round to see the lady who was about to become my wife. Even though her face was veiled in fine lace, I could see she was smiling, and her big blue eyes sparkled as she walked slowly down the aisle.

Minutes later Alex passed me the ring. It was the symbol of future happiness, a platinum band inset with diamonds. I placed it on Emma's slender finger, where it snuggled against the engagement ring created by the same craftsman. I loved her hands; they were gentle yet practical. She looked more beautiful than ever before.

My wedding band was equally special, because it was unique. On the outside it was a plain gold band, but on the inside was inscribed a verse from an Old Testament love story – the Song of Solomon, chapter 8, verse 6: "Set me as a seal upon your heart." With words that would touch my skin for evermore, she was saying to me: if you love me, your heart will be content; you will need nothing and no one else.

Dressed in a miniature ceremonial uniform, Harry held my Sword of Honour proudly above his head as we left the church. They stopped the traffic in the market town as our horse-drawn carriage made its way to the Spencer family's hotel. Children waved, men cheered and women commented on how beautiful the bride looked. I had everything I ever wanted.

In only five years, I would lose it all. Everything.

CHAPTER 18

Matty

Our first son, Matthew, was born nine months after our honeymoon. Emma continued to work at the hotel until just two weeks before Matty's birth. I left the house just after five each morning for the station and returned late every night. At the weekend, there were always jobs to do around the house we'd bought together, a big Victorian semi overlooking the town.

On Matthew's christening day, Emma and I had both been distracted by our beautiful ten-month-old son, and we were running late for the service. Gazing down at him, we couldn't resist one last little tickle, in spite of the time. "He's so beautiful, isn't he?" said Emma.

"Just like his mum. Now come on, or we're going to be late!"

But Emma was in one of her speculative moods. "It feels wrong, somehow," she mused as she applied the last touches of makeup to her face.

"What feels wrong?"

"To go to church, pretending we're good Christians. When was the last time we went to church? Christmas?"

She was right; we had both been so busy that church hadn't featured in our lives for some time. I knew I'd let my faith slip ever since I'd taken the new job, but I always felt I would get back into the habit when life calmed down a bit.

"Well, we can't miss this service. Come on, they'll be wondering where we are."

The church was full of friends and family. Matthew was presented with a lovely silver-bound Bible engraved with his name. Alex, who had done such a good job as best man, travelled all the way from Wales to be Matty's godfather, alongside my brother Duncan. I found myself imagining what would happen if Matthew took after his godfathers, becoming a huge rugby player.

Something about this thought troubled me. As with all parents, I noticed my son's key developmental milestones, just as I had noticed and remembered Harry's. Something about Matty was nagging at the back of my mind. Although Emma's parents laid on an amazing party for all our friends, I couldn't shake the uneasy feeling. It was like a dark cloud blocking out the sun, casting a shadow on the ground.

At ten months old, Matty wasn't crawling yet. Harry had been walking on his own by that stage. I said nothing, but something was also worrying me about the obvious way in which Matty favoured his left hand. There were no left-handers at all in my family. Still, there were left-handers in Emma's family: Matty's grandmother, and his great-grandfather and his cousins. I was probably worrying unnecessarily – another thing I shared with other parents. Maybe the dark clouds had other causes.

Life at home was so full of love that it was becoming harder and harder to drag myself out of the house to work each morning. My alarm would sound at a quarter to five. I had a thirty-minute drive to the station, which even my Porsche Cayenne struggled to make enjoyable these days, then a three-hour train journey before I even arrived at my desk. By the time I got back at night Matthew, and usually Emma too, would be asleep. More and more I needed a reason to remind myself why I made this daily journey. My enthusiasm for each day seemed to be diminishing, and with it, my ambition.

Furthermore, I had suffered some setbacks in work. The role I had been promised never materialized. I returned from my honeymoon to discover that the job had been given to someone else. Rather than make a fuss, I just accepted the fact that I was on a good wage and even if the job I was doing wasn't challenging, I would make the most of it. But inside I was hurting. I didn't receive many invitations to corporate events any more and when I did, my place was certainly not on the top table.

I had also suffered a more personal setback. My tough daily commute to work was worth it to live at home, and to be near to Harry, at last. I saw a lot of him now, and our weekends together were a huge source of joy to me. We were very close and as Harry celebrated each birthday, we only seemed to get closer. Like me, Harry lived for his sport and trained with the Birmingham Football Academy on Sundays. I loved to watch him play football. I used to love meeting the other fathers by the side of the pitch. But I will never forget the Sunday before Matty's christening. It was towards the end of the session and the boys were playing a game. As usual, the parents were getting into it as much as the boys, so it was slightly surprising when one of the other fathers, whom I didn't know well, took his eye off the game and came over to talk to me. It was cold and I remember feeling really grateful to him as he passed me a steaming cup of tea.

"I suppose you'll miss all this," he said, quite casually.

"Sorry?" I asked, not understanding what he meant.

"You know, when he goes to Jersey." He saw the look on my face. "Oh. You didn't know, then?" He looked embarrassed, but I didn't stay around to talk. I felt as though I had been run over by a bus. I was sure it was a mistake. Harry's stepfather had grown up in Jersey, but he hadn't lived there for some years. There had never been any discussion that he might go back there. I called my ex-wife's number.

"Is there something you need to tell me?" I asked.

After a long pause, she just said, "Like what?"

"Like you're taking Harry to live in Jersey."

"Oh, like that. Well, I didn't want to tell you until we were sure. How did you find out?"

"Some bloke on the side of the pitch just told me. I don't even know his name. Jersey's like another country. This is devastating. How could you?!"

"It's not that far. You can fly there quicker than you can catch a train to London."

"When are you going?"

"Next month. We have a house organized and James has a job with the bank... I'm sorry. I should have told you before."

That journey back home without Harry in the seat next to me was bleak. I realized that I would never take him to training again and that my weekends would be emptier without his company. I came very close to crying. The wounds from years before, that I thought had healed, had opened again and I was bleeding. But this time, I had a wife and another son waiting for me when I got home.

When I got back Emma was waiting to comfort me. She didn't say anything; she just hugged me and cried for me. We would all miss Harry. I went inside and scooped Matty up in my arms.

A week or so after Matty's christening, as I drove to the station, I caught an interview on the radio. It was with a famous footballer who had just retired. He explained that he was looking forward to spending more time with his daughter, who had recently been diagnosed with a form of cerebral palsy known as hemiplegia. The first thing her parents had noticed was that she favoured the use of her left hand. They thought she might be left-handed at first, but when she hadn't learned to crawl, they took her to see a doctor, and received a formal diagnosis.

I called Emma from the car phone. "I don't think Matty is left-handed. I think we should take him to see a specialist," I blurted.

"What are you talking about?" she said, in a sleepy voice.

"Have you ever heard of hemiplegia?"

Oddly, I felt slightly happier. Perhaps we had an answer to some of my concerns, and perhaps that answer would bring further answers.

My improved mood didn't last long, though. On the train that very morning, I received an email from the chief executive, announcing the latest round of promotions and inviting us all to congratulate all those on the attached list. My name was not one of those on the list. I felt that life was dealing me a tough hand. But there was even worse to come.

When we realized there could be a more sinister reason for the lack of dexterity in Matty's right hand, we took him for a private consultation at Great Ormond Street Children's Hospital. It only took a few minutes for the diagnosis. It took weeks before the shock subsided. The consultant referred us to a specialist in Derbyshire, who recommended a brain scan.

A few days later, Emma and I were staring at a screen at the hospital in Derby. *There must be some mistake*, I thought. *There is no way that is a picture of Matthew's brain!* I wanted to speak out loud, but I had to be strong for Emma, who was looking as shocked as I felt.

"Well, at least we know for certain now," I said, trying to sound positive.

"But it's so big, the scar – it covers a third of his brain." Emma gripped my hand tightly. I welcomed her touch. It reassured me.

"This is a cross-section at its most obvious. The scar probably looks worse than it is, but it is quite large. Yes, it is prominent," said the paediatric consultant.

"What caused it?" Emma and I asked at the same time.

"We can't be certain, but it is most likely that a blood clot formed and blocked a major blood vessel in his brain, causing the brain cells that the blood would have supplied oxygen to, to die. Matthew has suffered a stroke."

We had other questions. When was it caused? Could it have been prevented? How will it affect him? Will he walk? Will he talk? The consultant had few answers, but one thing she did say we will never forget: "There is an increased likelihood that Matthew will be prone to fits. He has a large lesion on his brain and this may well lead to unusual brain activity."

"You mean epilepsy?" asked Emma.

"Yes, but don't be alarmed. It may not manifest itself until he is much older – maybe never. But you just need to be aware that it could happen."

The weeks after the diagnosis were difficult. I was missing Harry and now the future looked bleak. Every parent has dreams for their children. We were coming to terms with the fact that our child was brain damaged and would probably need our care for the rest of his life. It wasn't that he would be loved any less, it was just that we had to adjust our view of the future, and it took time. I don't think Emma and I had ever argued before. But those first few weeks were quite tough. Outwardly it hit Emma hard. I tried to show very little emotion, but on the inside I was in turmoil.

Then, one day, the sun came out and things seemed brighter again.

"Well, come on. Tell me," I said impatiently.

"See for yourself!" Emma was smiling. It was so good to see her smile again. She showed me a small plastic stick on which two little blue lines were clearly visible. After a few months of trying, Emma was pregnant.

The news lifted us both. We loved Matty, but we knew life would be a challenge as he grew up. Now he would have a little sister or brother, and family life might be a little more normal. Over the next few weeks Emma blossomed. We talked about little else; it was such a relief to focus on something positive.

CHAPTER 19

Shocks

I was just about to start a round of golf with my brother Duncan and a business client at the London Club, one of the finest golf clubs in the south-east. We were waiting to tee off when I remembered my mobile. I needed to set the ring tone to vibrate only. As I was about to turn it off it rang loudly in my hand. It was Emma.

"I've had a bit of bleeding," she said. "Not much, but I'm worried."

"OK, well, if you're worried you should call the surgery and make an appointment. I'll come straight back after the round."

I didn't think I was too concerned at first, but I played so badly, I knew the call had upset me. By the ninth hole, I made some excuse about feeling unwell and left Duncan with my client and drove home.

Three weeks later we left Matthew at Emma's parents' and drove to a private clinic in Nottingham. There had been no more bleeding, but Emma was worried. She just felt something had changed. Our worst fears were realized during the ultrasound scan. There was no movement and when measurements were taken, the age of the tiny baby matched the date of Emma's bleed. We were both totally devastated, but Emma still had to endure the pain and indignity of the miscarriage.

The weeks and months passed and we began to come to terms with our new situation. I found that I could work just as efficiently from home as I could in the office and was able to be more hands-on as a father. If my work suffered at all, I hardly noticed. I was so delighted that Emma and I were together on the day Matty took his first step. Emma cried and I couldn't stop smiling. I think the smile would have lasted a week if we hadn't almost lost Matthew the following day.

It was late June and the weather was extremely hot. Matty had a cold and by the afternoon, he was sleepy and lethargic. All he wanted to do was cuddle up to me. He felt very hot to the touch, but I just put it down to the heat of the day. As soon as his right arm started to twitch, I knew he was fitting. "Emma, he's having a fit!" I called out and Emma came running. We had no idea what to do. We jumped into the car. Emma drove and I held Matty tightly to me. It was sweltering in the car, even with the air conditioning on. And it was market day in town, so the traffic was terrible.

"I can't feel his breathing, Emma. I think we need to call an ambulance." We made the call and drove back home, taking instructions from a very calm-sounding lady at the other end of the phone line. As Matty's lips turned blue, Emma relayed instructions to me. We had laid Matty out on the back seat of the car. Sweat was dripping down my face as I tipped his little head back, checked his tongue was forward and put my lips to his. I had been taught mouth-to-mouth resuscitation in the Army, but I never imagined I would one day be breathing for my own son. "What's taking them so long?!"

That was not a good day for an emergency. For some reason, the ambulance in Ashbourne was unavailable, so we had to wait while one was dispatched from Derby. Matthew had been fitting for half an hour. He was still twitching, and he had turned a worrying shade of purple and I was now breathing for him. In desperation I prayed.

"Please, God, don't take him from us! Please help!"

"OK, Justyn, let me have a little room." It was our neighbour John, a retired surgeon. His calm manner reassured us both. "He just needs to cool down a bit, so I'm going to loosen his top and undo the buttons. It's so hot, isn't it?" I couldn't believe he was chatting about the weather!

I really don't know if Matty would have made it if John hadn't been walking back from the shops when he was. In my desperation to look after Matty, I had done everything wrong. Our son was having a febrile fit caused by a rapid rise in his core body temperature – a combination of his fever and the heat of the day. By holding him close rather than letting the cool air get to his skin, I had certainly not helped. The ambulance finally arrived at the same time as a paramedics team, so now there were four people from the emergency services. Matty was quickly given a powerful shot as I held his hand. I jumped into the back of the ambulance; I just didn't want to let go of him. I left Emma with John and managed a wave as the doors closed.

I can't remember ever thanking John properly for what he did that day, and I recently learned that he died quite suddenly. I would love to have attended the service of celebration of his life. He had many friends and the big church was completely packed. I hope he'll be waiting in heaven for me, because I have a huge thank-you for him.

Matty seemed to come out of his fit in the ambulance, but he didn't regain consciousness until several long hours later. The fit had exhausted him and the powerful medication had sent him to sleep. While I waited for Matty to come round I fretted about further damage to his brain. I was so happy when, still in intensive care, he finally opened his eyes and smiled at me.

Every day since then Matty has taken medication morning and night to control his fits. We were warned that there might be behavioural side-effects from the medication and that he would probably need to take some form of medication for the rest of his life. Despite the powerful medicine, there have been several occasions when he has needed urgent hospitalization. Since that day, Emma and I have never really been able to sleep at night without one of us worrying that he might be slipping into a fit. We went out and bought audio sensors, movement sensors and TV monitors, but there is nothing as reassuring as the sound of his regular breathing, and Matty still shares a bed with Mum or Dad.

The hospital was well equipped to look after children, but there were few facilities for parents, and after two days of sitting on a hard chair by Matthew's bedside I was relieved when he was finally discharged. I was exhausted, physically and emotionally. I had concerns about Emma's ability to have any more children following the miscarriage, my career was going nowhere and I felt my eldest son Harry had been taken from me. Now I was adjusting to the fact that my youngest son's life was utterly fragile.

It was only a few weeks later that I did something I had never done before. Something I will regret for the rest of my life. I only spent £5, but it would cost me everything.

PART 4

The Beginning
of the End

.

*The safest road to Hell is the gradual one –
the gentle slope, soft underfoot, without sudden turnings,
without milestones, without signposts.*

C. S. LEWIS

Chapter 20

The First Bet

It was a stormy Saturday afternoon when I placed my first bet. I was forty years old and feeling sorry for myself. I didn't want to go out, but I didn't want to stay in. I was in a grouchy mood that day and short-tempered.

It had been a frustrating and draining week at work. When the senior role I thought would be mine had been taken by someone else, I was tasked instead with growing the business by generating new sales and energizing the team to look for new opportunities. The national sales staff were lovely people, but not particularly effective at selling. Early on, I had set them individual sales targets: an unpopular move. Now, after two years of trying to change the culture, I was exhausted. I had run out of ideas, energy and enthusiasm. I didn't really feel part of things. Despite some of my own individual successes, the lack of collective success reflected badly on me. A meeting with the whole team that week had not gone well. My pride told me that my team's failures were not my fault. What more could I do if people wouldn't listen?

I still occasionally received calls from recruitment agents. Some of the roles they offered would have been perfect, but none of them came close to the wage I was currently on. I was proud that I had made a success of every opportunity in my business career so far. It would have felt wrong to admit defeat and leave, especially for a lower-paid job.

Pride, for me, was destructive. It was preventing me from enjoying my work, preventing me from changing it. Pride was stopping me from getting that buzz I had always got from smashing my targets and exceeding expectations. Instead of invigorated and enthusiastic, I felt sorry for myself, worn out and grumpy.

On the Saturday afternoon in question, I was home alone. It was a weekend, but now Harry was hundreds of miles away and I wasn't part of his training scene any more. Emma was with Matty at her parents' house less than a mile away. They had recently sold the hotel. Having worked with them every day since leaving university, it was natural for Emma to continue to spend a lot of time with them. It really shouldn't have been a surprise to me. It really shouldn't have made me this grumpy. But it did. I wasn't part of that side of things either.

Fed up with pacing about the house, I stepped outside to get some air in between the squally showers. I had kept the garden at Suffolk neat and tidy, cutting the lawn twice a week in the summer and keeping the beds and borders free from weeds. But in contrast, I had neglected the garden in our marital home. It was overgrown and riddled with nettles and other perennial weeds. Fallen leaves lay piled in heaps where the wind had gathered and dumped them. What had once been a passion for me, I now saw as a chore. I really wasn't in the mood.

Blown towards me by the stiff wind, the sounds of a local rugby match reminded me of something else I was missing. If I stood on tiptoe, I could just see the tall, white posts that marked both ends of the pitch. I realized just how much I missed the fun of playing sport on Saturday afternoons, the camaraderie of being part of a team, the contact, the thrill of winning or the desperation of being beaten. I looked at my watch. We had satellite TV but not the sports channels, however it would only take a phone call to upgrade.

Five minutes later I was watching a Premiership rugby match in the lounge, a beer in my hand and logs on the open fire. As I settled back in my chair an advertisement on a panel by the side of the pitch caught my eye. The name was quite familiar and seemed to be the subject of an increasing number of adverts on TV and in the newspapers, but it had never meant anything to me before. I ran upstairs to find my laptop. It only took a few minutes to open the account, and they even matched my deposit with a free bet. My heart was beating because it felt wrong. Not morally wrong, but wrong to be so frivolous with my money. I'd always been more of a spender than a saver, but I never took risks with my money. I avoided the stock market because I felt I didn't know enough about it. The numbers on the screen confused me. I struggled to understand the difference between "backing" and "laying". What were all these decimal numbers next to the bet selections? It felt as though I'd just walked into a bar for the first time in a foreign country. All the locals knew each other, but I didn't even know the words to order a drink.

But I did know my rugby and somehow I managed to place a bet backing my team, Bath, to win. As the game progressed I felt involved. I was a part of it. More than just a spectator, I had money at stake, and perhaps my pride: "I may not know anything about betting, but I think I know who will win this game." The result was never in doubt; Bath scored early and dominated the game. When the final whistle went, I wasn't even sure that I'd put the bet on correctly, but sure enough, the account was credited and I doubled my money. *This is easy*, I thought to myself, *and it's just a bit of fun. I wonder what's on next?*

"Hi. Having fun?" Emma called from the front door. I snapped shut the lid of the laptop before she came into the room holding a sleepy Matthew in her arms.

"Yes, thanks. Was going to do some gardening, but I've been watching the rugby. Shall I make something to eat?" I asked, feeling my face redden with guilt.

"Mmm, I'm starving. I'll just deal with Matty and then come down. Why don't you open a bottle of wine?" she called as she climbed the stairs.

We had a lovely evening. It was an ordinary end to a day that changed my life forever.

I wasn't hooked immediately. I didn't spend all my time placing bets. In fact, it took several months before I realized I was betting every week. I loved sport, and the fact that I was now paying for the sports channel probably encouraged me to watch more sport on television. The problem was, if there was a game on TV, I wanted to place a bet so that I felt a part of the event. The slogan I kept hearing all the time was, "It matters more when there's money on it."

I didn't tell Emma I had put a bet on a particular game, even when we were both watching. She loves tennis and we both have our favourite players. She must have thought it a bit strange when I started to cheer for players I had never supported before. Of course, she didn't suspect me of gambling. Why should she? I'd never placed a bet before other than participating in a sweepstake at work, or maybe the Grand National, if someone placed the bet for me. I had never been to a high-street betting shop. The thought appalled me. And yet here I was at home, secretly betting on sports events. At first I won quite frequently, and if I lost it didn't matter because the bets were always small. I didn't doubt that I was in control.

My work became less and less inspiring. One day I explained to my boss that it wasn't efficient for me to travel in on the train; I could log in remotely and work from home. As the company was expanding rapidly, the possibility of a free desk in the office was enough to persuade them that my working from home was a good idea. I was set up for a home log-in. Without the commute to work, I had much more time at home and for a short while enjoyed a better quality of life.

This was a very happy time for Emma and me. We had come to terms with Matty's disability and I was able to share more of the parenting duties. I saw more of Emma than ever before and soon another baby was on the way. Although Emma had stopped working after the hotel was sold, we still had more than enough money to enjoy holidays and nice restaurants. I even managed to tidy the garden. I enjoyed placing a bet and then listening to the sport on the radio while I dug over the beds.

We decided to fit a new kitchen and redecorate. Emma's father project-managed the home refurbishment, which soon included a new bathroom, wall-to-wall shelving and a brand-new heating system. When the project escalated in cost, I simply paid all the bills. But I was not hitting my targets at work, and although I was no longer getting bonuses I didn't admit to Emma that we ought to cut down our spending. Again my pride got in the way. The final bill cleared the last penny from my savings account. For the first time in a very long while there were no savings in the bank. I didn't tell Emma because I was feeling guilty about my betting.

One Monday morning in late autumn I was feeling restless. Work was slow and my in-tray was empty. Normally I would have made a few speculative calls, but I knew Emma was out for the day and that a tennis tournament had just started. There was full coverage of the games on two channels. I made a coffee and decided I would just sit and watch for a while. While I watched I decided to check my betting account. I hadn't really explored all the different parts of the website. I thought I had a feel for how much I was spending, but didn't really know the exact figures. Now that I had some time, I found the account page. I was shocked. I was £700 down.

A new match was just about to start. I looked at the odds for the player I thought should win. Then I calculated how much of a stake I would need to place to win back everything I had so far lost. I needed about £1,000. I didn't have that much in my account, but I wasn't overdrawn, so I rang my bank and arranged a £5,000 overdraft. It wasn't difficult. For the bank I was a safe bet; I was a home owner with a good wage. I immediately transferred £1,000 into my betting account and quickly placed the bet, blocking all the rational, logical warning thoughts out of my mind.

Placing the bet, I experienced a nervous feeling, like butterflies in my tummy. It was the same feeling I used to get in the back of a C-130 Hercules, when the parachutists' jump light changed from red to green. I had jumped. This was the biggest bet I had ever placed. Losing would be quite devastating, but if I won, I could close down my account in the knowledge that I hadn't lost anything. I could just forget this stupid activity that was the only secret between me and my wife; that was distracting me from work and making me miserable. I would be able to go for walks again and enjoy the countryside; enjoy playing with Matthew without wondering what sport was on.

Betting had become like an irritable itch. It wasn't painful, just uncomfortable, and the only way I had any relief was to scratch at it. Occasionally it would go away for a few days, but then I'd feel the itch again and have another scratch at it. If I won this bet, the itch would go away forever. This bet was different, though. I wasn't betting for fun; I was chasing my losses. I knew it was dangerous, but I had placed the bet before I allowed myself any logical thoughts.

Things were looking good to start with. My player won the first set and was a break up in the second. But then he seemed to lose concentration and he lost the next four games in a row, gifting the second set to his opponent. I couldn't watch. I kept standing up and pacing the room. My phone went, but I ignored it. I made another coffee, my heart beating rapidly as the kettle came to the boil.

When I lost that bet I experienced feelings that were new to me. I felt self-loathing. How could I have been so stupid? I also felt anger that someone had taken *my* money, money I could have spent on my family, on a holiday or a present for Emma. And I felt depressed. My life that had once been so good, so successful and fulfilled, was now reduced to this: secretly betting at home on a Monday morning, watching TV when everyone else was working hard to earn an honest wage. I hated those feelings. I could hardly bear another second of such self-loathing. I looked about desperately for anything that would restore my equilibrium and somehow give me back my self-respect and a sense of normality.

The commentator was announcing the next game. As soon as I placed that second big bet, the dark feelings left me and were instantly replaced with hope. I felt alive again, the adrenaline was pumping through me, my parachute was on, and we were nearing the drop zone. This time I was sure to win. Ever the optimist, I settled back to watch. What a great way to spend a Monday morning! Everyone else was at work, slaving away. I could make money and enjoy myself at home.

CHAPTER 21

The Gentle Slope

We were shopping. Emma held up a pair of shoes she thought might be suitable for Matty. "How about these?" she asked.

I only noticed the price tag. "I'm not sure I like the colour." I selected a pair £10 cheaper. "What about these?"

Emma looked surprised at my choice. "They look like trainers; he needs a smart pair for nursery."

I was cross about the shoes and I was cross about the nursery too. The fees were as expensive as any school I knew of. Emma and I had argued over it several times. All of her friends were sending their children to the private nursery, even though it was miles outside town. She had never been materialistic; she never asked me to buy her clothes or asked for money to go shopping with her friends. But she did want the best for her child. I couldn't tell her the real reason behind my objection to the nursery's costs. The truth was, I couldn't really afford it.

I sold my Porsche. I told Emma it was silly to drive a big car that guzzled fuel. Trusting my judgment, she didn't quiz me about my change of heart. It had never mattered before that the tyres didn't last long, or that they cost £200 each to replace, I still had a good income; I should have been able to run the car easily. But now I was regularly gambling secretly. I stood on the pavement outside our house for several minutes after the Porsche had disappeared around the corner. All I was left with was a key-ring, a set of out-of-date navigation disks and the smell of exhaust fumes. The car held some special memories for me, but I traded it in for a more practical estate model.

Having less money in my account should have made me feel less inclined to gamble. Instead it had the opposite effect. I wanted to keep gambling, in search of the big win that would allow me to pay off some of the credit card debt. I had to pay my own travel costs to the office, so I made the journey less frequently. I now had more time at home and more opportunities to gamble.

I played my cards close to my chest. I should have talked it through with Emma, but I didn't. I couldn't. I missed several opportunities to show her my hand. One night I stayed up in my office. I must have fallen asleep at my desk because she came to find me and saw the screen. When she confronted me I told her it was just a bit of fun, that my stakes were tiny. I could tell she was worried about me, but I wasn't willing to admit to myself that what I was doing was very dangerous. I still saw it as harmless fun, even though it was already having an effect financially, and probably emotionally.

I discovered horse racing by accident. I was looking forward to a cricket match in South Africa. The match wasn't televised, but I found a website with ball-by-ball commentary. I placed my bet and settled down with a cup of tea. Cricket matches might not appear to offer much for gamblers, but in fact, as the recent match- and spot-fixing scandals demonstrate (fuelled by massive underground syndicates in Asia), cricket can be very engaging for those who enjoy a bet. On my screen, I could bet for or against more than 200 different outcomes, including the number of runs scored in the first over, the first wicket to fall, the overall score, the runs scored by each batsman, the next batsman out, as well as the outcome of the match and the winning margin.

Five minutes before the start, my adrenaline levels were high and my heart was pounding. But something was wrong. The covers were still on. It was raining and the match was delayed. I felt like an Olympic runner, standing at the start of the race. I had prepared all year for this moment and all my energy was focused on the sprint ahead, and now I was told the race was delayed. With so much nervous energy to release, I couldn't just sit down and pick up the newspaper or make a few work calls. I had to run.

That's when I found the horse racing.

I backed the favourite and won. I didn't know anything about racing. I had no idea about form or distances. But that day I backed a couple of the favourites. I lost a few, but won more. The best thing was that if you lost one race, you could try and win your money back just a few minutes later. Racing was on most days and the race times were staggered to allow people to bet on each race sequentially. Most of the races were streamed live through the internet. They only lasted a few minutes, so the intensity of the bet seemed more concentrated, the adrenaline rush much greater than a ninety-minute football match.

Racing began just after lunchtime and could continue on until 9 p.m. Then the racing started in America, and when that was finished there was more racing in Australia. My website gave me access to every race. Betting on horses was a significant development in my gambling because it meant that I was glued to the computer in my office upstairs for longer periods.

It also meant more lies.

I explained my extended desk-time to Emma by lying that I was involved in important international conference calls. I asked not to be disturbed and so she left me alone. She was wonderfully supportive. Her love and trust made me feel guilty, unworthy and a cheat. I felt like a fraud when I came down the stairs to find a beautiful home-cooked meal on the table. Emma made time to cook, despite looking after a very demanding toddler and being several months pregnant. Normally I would have eaten the meal with her and asked her about her day, or planned an adventure for the weekend, but increasingly I was wolfing down the food and then rushing back upstairs to my office to place another bet. Sometimes I was happy at mealtimes and on these occasions I would linger at the table, chat to Emma, ask about her day and help to feed Matthew. At other times I was morose, reluctant to talk, and impatient to get back to my office. It all depended on how the last bet had worked out.

On the day the town switched on its Christmas lights I wasn't feeling in a festive mood. The first Friday in December was normally a happy time, one of the first indicators that Christmas was on the way. I usually felt childlike excitement in the lead-up to the festive season. But this year, for the first time in my life, the prospect of Christmas shopping made me panic.

December rolled us relentlessly forward towards Christmas. I was borrowing heavily and there were still a few presents to buy. It had become a tradition for me to give Emma an expensive handbag. I didn't want this year to be any different. I didn't want her to think I had any financial problems and I didn't want my family to suffer because I placed losing bets. Although worried about the cost of Christmas, I was happy because Harry was coming to stay for a week. He loved soldiers and miniature models, so I had decided to build him a "landscape" where we could set up his soldiers and play imaginary battles against each other. Building Harry's present also gave me an excuse to stay up late every evening in the run-up to Christmas Day, after Emma had gone to bed.

That was when I discovered darts.

Betting on darts gave me the same adrenaline rush as horse racing. You could bet on the outcome of games as well as the score and place many other in-play bets. There was a huge televised tournament with games every day in the run-up to Christmas and then on into the New Year.

Each evening, I became more and more excited, and impatient for Emma to go to bed so I could turn the darts on and place my bets. I offered to run her a bath and encouraged her to relax in bed. I resented any invitations to carol services or other evening social events that might conflict with the darts. At a time when most families joined together for the festive season, I sought solitude.

Emma probably thought I was trying to be a good father by giving up my evenings to build Harry's present.

But I wasn't.

Even after Christmas when Harry arrived for his holiday, I was distracted from being a good father and husband. Harry had always loved to watch ghost films. Even though he was still quite young, he was never scared as long as I was there with him. If there was a particularly creepy bit, he just closed his eyes and buried his head in my chest. One evening there was a film he wanted to watch. Emma hates anything spooky on TV, so she went to bed, leaving Harry and me to watch the film in the den next to the kitchen. I discovered that if I repositioned the furniture in the den and left the door to the kitchen open, I could sit on the sofa and watch the film with Harry, while being able to see the darts on the TV in the kitchen.

Poor Harry. He couldn't understand why his dad had suddenly taken a liking to darts, or why I kept rushing upstairs to do something on the computer. At one point, as the film reached its scary climax, I left to place a bet despite Harry pleading with me to stay. When I came down I found him in tears. I hadn't been there for him to cuddle up to and he had been really scared. It shook me immensely. I woke the next morning and firmly resolved to stop betting. I cancelled my sports TV subscriptions and closed down my betting account.

I began the New Year feeling positive. I spent more time with Emma and Matthew, I had a renewed energy for work and even my financial situation improved. For a few weeks, I felt so much better about life.

And then Alex invited me to the Millennium Stadium in Cardiff to watch a rugby international. I loved rugby; watching the game live, in what is probably the best stadium in the UK, was always an amazing treat. In the week before the game, I began to think how much more fun it would be if I were to place a bet before I left for

Wales. How could it hurt to have one bet? But something held me back. I wrestled with the urge to scratch my itch. I seemed to be holding out. I had no intention of betting.

Then, on the morning of the game, I simply logged in to check my emails... There was one from the betting company. I shouldn't have opened it, but I did. They told me they hadn't seen me for a while and as a special gift they offered me a free bet, as long as I made a small deposit. I didn't stand a chance. It only took five minutes to re-open the account and place my bet. I lost so much more than my stake that day. I lost my self-respect and soon I was back into a pattern of chasing my losses and betting to escape the self-loathing I felt.

CHAPTER 22

Out of Control

Emma was worried about me. She could see that I was unhappy, and as a loving wife she was desperate to understand why. She frequently suggested things that would lift my mood and get me out of the house. She understood that I was dissatisfied at work and asked me if I would consider moving jobs, but I liked the fact that I was well paid and could work from home. Both suited my gambling. By now, I was willing to admit to myself that the gambling was a habit, but I was not yet ready to admit that it was an addiction.

Before Christmas Emma had said to me, "I think living in a town is making you sad. I think we should move back to the country. I know you aren't happy and I know how much you love the countryside." I had agreed to call an estate agent after the Christmas holiday and get our property valued. I kept that promise.

As spring approached, I was gambling more than ever. As usual, I was in my office at home, glued to a tennis match on my computer screen. When I heard Emma climbing the stairs, I quickly closed down the betting page. The work page I had set up behind it sprang to life before she peered around the office door. "Justyn," she said with a look of desperation on her face, "we've run out of orange-flavoured biscuits. Could you pop out and get some?" She was eight months pregnant: I could hardly refuse her craving request.

A car honked loudly as I stepped onto the busy road next to the marketplace. I was now avidly following the tennis match on my BlackBerry, and it was the final set. There were dozens of mobile websites showing live results; this one seemed to update its pages more often than the others, giving a potential advantage when you were betting in play. It was a particularly tight game.

Still in one piece, I managed to look up as I crossed the busy street. I recognized a friendly face waiting for me on the other side. "Hello, Justyn – that was a close one! How are you?" It was the father of one of Emma's close friends. I knew he lived in France, but I couldn't quite remember his name.

"Yes," I laughed, a bit embarrassed. "I was checking my emails. Can't escape work anywhere now!" I shoved the BlackBerry into my pocket. "Are you over for a holiday?"

"Sort of – we're actually house-hunting. We've decided to move back."

Momentarily I forgot the tennis match. I was finding it harder to meet the monthly mortgage payments and the idea of selling our house was becoming quite appealing. I invited him for a coffee and was pleased to discover they were looking for a townhouse. Our home had just been valued and was in their price range. Following our refurbishment, the house looked at its best in the early spring sunlight. They made an offer that morning, for the full amount. They were keen to move in and we wanted to find a new place before the baby was born, so we rented a beautiful cottage in the countryside. When the sale went through, the equity was transferred to my account.

Oscar was born within a week of our move, and he was gorgeous. It was spring and, like our little boy, everything was new and fresh. Although it was always the intention to buy another house, we loved this cottage. A little stream ran alongside it, and in the front garden was a beautiful cherry tree, covered in blossom. As I parked the car under the delicate white petals, with our little baby wrapped up snugly on the back seat, I decided once more to make a fresh start. I used some of the house equity to clear my debts and for a few weeks I felt as light-hearted as if we were all on holiday.

But I didn't close down my betting account and there was a large lump sum sitting in my bank. It wasn't very long before I made up my mind to try and win back all I had lost. I couldn't stop thinking about the money I'd squandered. I just wanted to win it back. But this was different. Up to that point, the money I'd risked had been all mine – well, mine and the bank's. That was no longer the case. Most of the equity in our house had come from the sale of Emma's first house. She had worked so hard and poured all her savings into that house. Now she trusted me to invest sensibly and look after it for the sake of the family. She trusted me with all the finances because I worked in the financial sector and should really know about money.

This time, with access to more money, my stakes were larger. When I won, I won sizable amounts, but when I lost, I kept chasing, trying to win back money that wasn't really mine. It felt wrong to be using Emma's money, but I managed to convince myself that I was just investing it in a high-risk strategy and that I could and would win it all back. Occasionally she asked to see a statement, but I made some excuse. As looking after Matthew was such an intense occupation, her requests were soon forgotten. We never ever sat down and went through a budget or talked about money.

When I lost I felt angry that someone else was taking money from me and my family. The motivation to continue to gamble came from my need to replace the money before Emma found out it was missing. I could see no other way of covering my tracks. But it also sickened me that I had allowed us all to get into this position. I still held on to my optimistic outlook, so I didn't ever dwell on the negative thoughts for long. Instead, each morning I sat at my desk at home and while the computer warmed up, I convinced myself that this would be the day I would win everything back. Before long, the equity that would have been a good deposit on a new home had dwindled.

One warm midsummer day I was in the office at home. All the windows were open, allowing a cool breeze to blow through the little room. Outside, house martins swooped and dived, chasing after juicy flies, while puffy white clouds drifted slowly across the clear blue sky. From the office I had a lovely view across green fields and up towards a small range of hills from which, on a clear day like today, you could see five different counties. Although I loved the country, I hardly ever left the office except when I was needed in London.

Something made me glance up from the screen. I could see Emma coming up the lane; Matty was running ahead, throwing sticks and leaves into the little stream that ran past our house. She was pushing Oscar in his little buggy and she was happy. I could see her lovely smile even from a distance. Minutes later she called up to the open window.

"I think I've just found our dream home!"

She wanted me to drop everything and come for a walk. Her enthusiasm was contagious. I left what I was doing and followed her, making sure I kept my phone to hand. The lane followed the course of the stream and today it looked at its very best, the green hedgerows alive with songbirds. After about a mile the lane ended near a duck pond that Matty loved to visit. This had been the site of a huge stately home. Like many other country houses, between the two world wars it had fallen into disrepair and was pulled down in the 1930s. There were a number of lovely old stone farmhouses near the duck pond, but the "For Sale" sign seemed to be attached to the tall wall that enclosed what would once have been the kitchen garden for the country house. It was not clear which house was for sale.

I followed Emma through a series of gates and then through a small door in the old brick wall giving access to the kitchen garden. I had to duck and then blinked in the bright sunshine; it felt as though I had just stepped into a little piece of paradise. There were orchards, manicured lawns, beautifully tended borders, ancient-looking wooden glass-houses, vines, rose-beds and expertly trained fruit trees growing all along the insides of the walls. Chickens, ducks and geese roamed freely between the shrubs. The cottage was right in the middle and not visible from outside the wall. My eye was led naturally along the course of a path down to an archway in the lower wall and out across field after green field. It took my breath away.

"What a view!" I said, shielding my eyes from the midday sun.

"I thought you'd like it." Emma was smiling broadly. "The cottage is called Distant Point. Come and see it." She was skipping now. I almost joined in.

I did like it. I felt my heart thudding. I could imagine the boys growing up there. I could grow fruit and vegetables, restore the old glass-houses, and we could keep chickens. There was plenty of room for pigs too. It had always been our dream to live a country life. Soon we were approached by a lovely old lady, bent double with age, but her smiling face shone and she had the complexion of someone much younger. She loved watching Matty chase the chickens. After inviting us in for tea she explained why she was selling up. Since her husband had passed away, she had been finding it harder to keep the place as it should be. The time had come for her to move closer to her daughter in Sheffield.

The price she was asking was very reasonable and only a little more than we had just sold our house for. It should have been very affordable. For a few minutes, as we explored the garden, I was lost in the excitement of the moment. I noted the best trees for a swing for the boys; I even planned the crop rotation. And then I remembered the reality of the situation. I felt as though I'd just fallen out of one of the apple trees and landed in chicken poo.

Emma talked of little else over the next few days, and went back to visit Distant Point with her parents, who, unsurprisingly, loved it at first sight. I called my bank in desperation. Although we could quite easily have a mortgage, we needed a deposit. The original amount from the sale of our house would have been just enough to secure affordable financing on my wage. There was no chance of a mortgage without the deposit. I felt completely and totally devastated, but I had no way of telling Emma how I felt. Later that day I went back with Emma and this time I pointed out to her all the drawbacks. It needed work, access for a vehicle was difficult, and the mains utilities were antiquated. They were all things we could happily have overcome, but now I made them out to be show-stoppers. I watched my wife as she visibly deflated. What had been pure excitement turned into a deep sadness. She'd been happy, not just for herself, but also for me and the boys. She knew we would have been happy there. Walks to the duck pond were forever sad after that day. It wasn't long before the "For Sale" sign was taken down and somebody else's removal lorries carrying somebody else's furniture arrived.

It was to be the first of several houses Emma found that would have fulfilled all our dreams. Each time I followed the same pattern. I visited the house and showed enthusiasm, but then on the second viewing, I found some fault or other. "Too close to the road... Too far from a school... The pond's a bit dangerous... There aren't enough bedrooms... The garden's too small... The garden's too big." Each time I had to watch as Emma's dreams and hopes were dashed. It was a cruel thing to do; something that I will always regret. I tried to justify it by convincing myself that all the faults in these houses were genuine; that the cottage we were renting was lovely and we didn't need to be buying a house at a time when house prices were falling. But the fundamental reason why we couldn't move house was that my gambling had damaged our financial position. I hated myself for the lies.

CHAPTER 23

Autism

It wasn't just our finances I was destroying; our relationship was suffering too. We never really argued before I began gambling, but now we argued regularly. My mood swings were difficult for Emma, who was struggling to cope with Matty each day. As he grew older, we noticed his behaviour was different from that of other children his age. The way he lined up all his toys in one long line seemed slightly eccentric. Staff at the nursery were also noticing how obsessive he was about certain things and how hard he found it to interact with the other children.

I'd been in London all day and by the time I drew up outside the cottage it was quite late.

"Hi. Are you still up?" I called as I opened the door, not quite loud enough to wake any sleeping children. There was no reply, but I could hear the faint sound of sobbing coming from the lounge. I put my briefcase down and walked through the open-plan kitchen and dining room. The lights were off in the lounge, but there was enough light to see the half-empty bottle of wine on the side table.

"What's the matter?" I asked as I sat down next to Emma and put my arm around her. She had curled up in a protective ball and her cheeks were wet and shiny.

"Oh, Justyn, it's so awful..."

"What is? What's so awful?" (*This is it*, I thought. *She's found out.*)

"It's Matty. The nursery staff think he might be autistic and one of the other mothers has taken her daughter to another nursery because she was scared of Matthew. He's been hitting the other children," she said as the tears came. "Haven't we had enough to deal with already? Hemiplegia, epilepsy and now this?"

I held her tightly and stroked her long hair. She was normally so strong, always looking for any form of silver lining. But now she seemed broken and vulnerable. I loved her completely. It seemed strange that I could be hiding a habit that would have devastated her if she had known about it, and yet I still adored her; she was the centre of my universe. I hated myself, and that prevented me from showing her the affection she deserved and needed. But I loved her more than ever.

Within a week Matthew was diagnosed. It had been suspected by the various professionals who interacted with him each week: his speech and language therapist, his occupational therapist and his physiotherapist. Once we had the diagnosis, it seemed somehow easier. We were given coping strategies and visual aids to help us with getting him dressed, and with his eating and bedtime. What made it worse was that Oscar was copying many of Matty's extreme behavioural traits.

Mealtimes were a trial. Matty often regurgitated his food as though it were all a game. One particular incident stands out. It was Matthew's third birthday party and we invited all his friends. Matty was at the head of the table and had just eaten a huge plate of fish fingers, beans and chips. While all the other guests were still eating, the birthday boy decided to bring his entire meal (in a rather more mushed state) back onto his paper plate. Stunned into silence, the children and parents stared in horror as Matthew gagged again and again, laughing heartily as he went.

Everyday life had become a huge strain. My stress levels were close to breaking point as my losses mounted. Soon all the money was gone and I began to borrow again to maintain our lifestyle. A large proportion of my wage was now disappearing on loan repayments. My credit cards were maxed out, as was my overdraft, and the bank had just refused me any more credit.

Christmas was approaching fast and I was really dreading it. One Friday, a few weeks before Christmas, I was driving back from the station when Emma called.

"Are you nearly home?" she asked.

"Yes, about twenty minutes."

"Great. Father Christmas is at the farm shop. Matthew really wants to see him. We've written a letter and everything."

Oh no, it's not payday till Tuesday, I thought. I knew I just about had enough in my account for fuel and groceries. I had to avoid any additional expense. So I waited five minutes and then called her back.

"Hey you. Traffic's a nightmare. I think there must have been an accident ahead. Why don't you go on ahead and I'll catch you up?" The lies came more easily now.

"OK. I might give my parents a call – I'm low on cash. Come as soon as you can, or you'll miss the fun."

A quarter of an hour later I drove up to the house cautiously. Emma's father was just loading Matthew into the back seat, so I carried on past, hoping no one had spotted my car. I let myself into the house after they had left. I wasn't sure how much longer I would be able to go on before something had to give. I knew the day would come when I would have to tell Emma what had happened to the money. Perhaps things would have come to a head that Christmas, but then an opportunity came along for me to put everything right.

Emma had worked for the family business from the day she left university. When you sit down and enjoy a meal at a good restaurant, you don't realize how hard people are working to make the business a success. The hours are long, the guests can be demanding and there are always staff issues to deal with. Before Matthew was born, the only time I ever got to see Emma at the weekends was when I helped by serving at the hotel bar. Friday and Saturday nights, Sunday lunchtimes and Bank Holidays were the busiest times. Weddings were the hardest of all. By midnight I would be exhausted, but often this was when Emma had to kick into another gear as she sent her staff home and took over without complaining. Very often, she would work through the night, come home for an hour or so and then go back to help with breakfast and check-out.

When the family sold the hotel, Emma, as one of the directors, was entitled to a share of the proceeds of the sale. When the money arrived, Emma asked me if I would invest it with the money from the sale of our house. This, I knew, was an opportunity to stop gambling. I had no intention of using any more of Emma's money. We might have lost the money from the sale of our house, but this would be enough to put down a deposit on a new house. I could also borrow against it and clear or reschedule my debts, allowing us enough money each month to live within our means. Even when the darts championship started, I resisted the urge to place any bets. After all, while I could have argued that some of the equity from the sale of our house was legitimately mine, this was all Emma's money. It would be so wrong to touch it in any way.

I felt an overwhelming sense of relief that we had money in the bank. When my brother asked if we would join his family for a few days at our favourite hotel in Devon, I didn't hesitate. The hotel in Thurlstone is a family-run place, with excellent facilities for children. We had a lovely time. All financial worries were put to one side and we relaxed, went for long walks along the dramatic coastline and pampered ourselves in the health club.

However, on the last morning, I did a quick calculation and realized my debit card might not authorize the hotel payment, due to lack of funds. I didn't want any embarrassment, so I put in a quick call to my bank to transfer some money from the savings account where Emma's money was earning interest. It was a long journey back to Derbyshire and while Emma and the boys slept, I had time to contemplate what I had done. I felt guilty for using her money, but then I tried to justify it in my mind because we had all had such a great time. There really was no justification. What I had done was wrong and I knew it.

The following day I opened the newspaper and read about the Ashes cricket tour taking place in Australia. My eye was drawn to the familiar brand being advertised next to the match report. Having used some of Emma's money the previous day, I had already broken my own rules. It was now much easier to transfer a small amount into my account, thinking I would just try and win back the cost of our recent hotel break.

The next few weeks were a crazy and gluttonous indulgence in gambling. Once more, I was chasing my losses, desperate to win back what I had lost. After a month I was down to the last £10,000 of Emma's money. It was the opening weekend of the Six Nations Rugby Championship. Deliberately I numbed my mind to the thought of what I was doing by drinking heavily. Blocking out any consideration of what might happen if I lost, I placed half the remaining money on England to win the opening game. They won comfortably.

I knew what was at stake. If I lost all of Emma's money, my marriage would probably be over. If I won back what I had lost, I had the chance to reinstate our savings account, close down the betting account and put this awful chapter in my life behind me without anyone knowing. I took it very seriously. Each morning I carefully scanned the papers for sporting events where I might be able to predict the outcome. I avoided events I knew little about. I went running each morning to clear my head and keep myself fit. I avoided drinking alcohol when I was betting to make sure I had all my wits about me. Slowly, I began to win more than I was losing, but there was a cost. I became even more reclusive. Emma and I had always enjoyed dinner parties with friends. Now, if we received an invitation, I encouraged Emma to go on her own, telling her that we couldn't both leave Matthew.

It was around this time that Matty had another serious fit. When I think back, every significant event, anniversary, holiday or birthday at that time seems to be linked in my mind with a particular bet I had placed. As usual, Matthew was sleeping between us in our bed. We had long since given up on the TV monitor because any noise or movement made us jump and fret until one of us went to check on him. Moving Matthew into our bed seemed to improve Emma's sleep, but I hadn't enjoyed a good night's sleep for many months – a combination of a bad conscience and the adrenaline highs of high-risk gambling for several hours each day.

It was just before five on the fifth anniversary of our wedding day. It was still very dark outside and I was awake. Before I went to bed I had laid up a tray for Emma with a card and a present. I never forgot the anniversary of the best day of my life and had a few surprises lined up for her. I was about to discover that Matthew had a surprise of his own lined up for us both. I felt Matthew's right arm begin to spasm in a now-familiar, jerking way; softly at first, and then more urgently.

"Emma." I wasn't whispering, but I also didn't want to panic her or frighten Matty, who often came round on his own quite naturally. She was deeply asleep, so I called her name a little louder, turning on the lamp on my side of the bed while I did so.

"He's just started jerking." I lifted one of his closed eyelids. "Eyes round to the right."

"OK, let's keep calm and see if he comes round." Her voice was reassuring. We had both been there before, but we were aware that about one in three of these fits would mean a high-speed ambulance ride to intensive care.

"Matty, Matty…" I spoke gently and touched his shoulder. Shaking him would do no good and might make things worse. "He's not coming out of it. Have you got the Buccolam?" Emma kept a syringe of buccal midazolam to hand near her bedside. If Matty didn't come round on his own after a few minutes, we gave him the prescribed dose orally.

"Give it another minute. How's his breathing?"

Emma was rightly reluctant to hold off from giving him the strong medication; it really knocked him out and meant we had to call an ambulance. There was still a chance he would come out of the fit on his own. But after another minute there was no improvement.

"No change. Breathing's getting shallower. Let's go for it," I said. "I'll call the ambulance."

Fifteen minutes later, a blue flashing light filled the room, indicating that either the first responders were outside, or the ambulance crew. The Buccolam was very powerful and normally Matthew would have come round, at least intermittently, by the time the first vehicle arrived. But this time, he was still in a fit when the cheery first responder crew appeared. Matthew was violently sick. This was nothing new, but it was also dangerous, because we now had no idea how much of the medicine he had ingested.

"Morning, Matthew. Are you keeping your parents up again?" The first responders lived locally and knew Matthew well. It wasn't the first time they had been called out to us in the middle of the night. There was no response from Matthew. Efficiently they attached an instrument to his finger to monitor his heart rate and, more importantly, the oxygen level in his blood. Without prompting, Emma gave them the time he had gone into the fit, the time she had administered the medication, and confirmed the dosage. If Matthew had to go into hospital it always meant an overnight stay. There was no sense of panic, but instinctively I headed through to the office where I kept my clothes.

As I was packing my bag, I heard the arrival of the paramedic crew. In one room, my son's life hung in the balance as he struggled with a deep and dangerous epileptic fit. In the next room, I suddenly remembered that I had placed a bet on two tennis matches in the Australian Open that were taking place overnight, UK time. Without really thinking what I was doing, I turned the computer on. With my bag packed, I quickly loaded up my betting account. I was looking to see if my balance had been credited, which would indicate I had won the bet. I was disappointed that my balance was exactly the same as it had been the previous evening. Not the end of the world; it might just mean the bets hadn't been settled. It took a minute to find my favoured results page and, sure enough, both games had gone to fifth and final sets. My heart was already racing with the urgency of Matty's situation; it now beat even faster.

I grabbed my phone and took my bag through to the bedroom, which was now crowded with two first responders, two paramedics and an ambulance crew. The room was full to capacity with fluorescent yellow-and-green uniforms and all the associated equipment. This was a wedding anniversary we would never forget, and definitely not for the romance of the occasion.

"How's he doing, Emma?" I asked.

"His oxygen levels are a bit low, but look – he's with us again, Just."

"We'll have to take him in; I'm a little concerned about the blood oxy level." The paramedic sounded more worried than usual.

"OK, I'm ready to go." I pointed to my bag. "Matty, we're going in a nee-nah. You are so-o-o lucky! I'll call you later, Em."

She kissed Matthew as we carried him out to the back of the ambulance. As I walked through the kitchen I glanced at the tray I'd laid the night before, with a red rose in a small glass vase and the teapot I had carefully wrapped in heart-patterned paper. Matthew had wet himself and was not in good shape. I also knew that the twenty-five-minute trip in the ambulance normally sent him back into his fit. Sure enough, his eyes kept flicking back to the right, an indication that he was still fitting.

"I'm going to give him some more Buccolam – but that's really all we can do for him now," said the paramedic.

I held Matty's hand as we sped off towards Derby hospital, lights flashing and siren blasting out as the residents of Ashbourne woke up to a new day. And in my other hand I held my mobile. The display showed that I had lost one of the matches, but was up in the other.

Chapter 24

Toilet Brushes

For the first time in a year and a half, I could breathe freely again. I sucked in the cool morning air as I jogged back down the hill towards home. It had been a tough ascent, but now I was rewarded by a stunning view across southern Derbyshire and out towards Staffordshire. I could see Cannock Chase in the distance and, beyond that, the hills of Shropshire and the Welsh borderland. Mist had gathered in the hollows and valleys, but this was evaporating rapidly as the late-winter sun climbed above the horizon. I hadn't really taken the time to appreciate the beauty of our location, but now this run was part of my daily routine.

Before I set off that morning, I checked my betting account balance. I had £73,000 in the pot. It had taken me about six weeks to win back most of the money. On average now I was winning about £1,000 a day, sometimes more. I was sticking to events I felt I knew something about. I kept away from horse racing and on the days when I didn't win, I just accepted it, cut my losses and looked forward to the following day. This was manageable. It wasn't hard; I wondered how I'd been so unlucky before. I only had another £23,000 to win, and then I would quit. Or perhaps not. *I'm getting rather good at this*, I thought to myself. *When I've won all Emma's money back, I'll transfer it into a separate savings account and perhaps just keep a few thousand to play with.*

I was on a winning streak and full of confidence. "Perhaps I'll just take a look in the paper this morning and see what horses are running today," I mumbled to myself as home came back into view. "It won't hurt to have a look; there may be a dead cert."

That was the last day I went for a run.

I lost money on the horses, but I was convinced I had been really unlucky. I backed a horse that would have won me a lot of money. Approaching the final furlong, it was way out in front and not even tiring. It fell at the last fence.

I hated the feeling. I didn't want to end the day down, having come so close to being up. So I surfed some internet sites and found a tennis match. It was a game between the world number one, Victoria Azarenka, and a rank outsider, some 200 places lower than her in the world rankings table. The odds were very weak. I calculated that to win back the money I had lost and to show a small profit, I would have to place a bet of £17,000 backing Azarenka to win. To place the bet, I would need to call the gambling company and get them to lift any restrictions on the size of bet I could place. It didn't take long; no questions were asked. They never were. In fact, I was asked if I wanted my own VIP account director to look after me and take all my bets. Around this time, I was also asked if I wanted to attend sporting events as a guest of the betting company. I hardly thought twice as I casually placed the largest bet of my life. Azarenka cruised through the first set and I was so confident I would win the bet that I agreed to go shopping with Emma while the game was still in play.

We were in Homebase about an hour later. We needed to buy a toilet brush, but couldn't find them. I left Emma to search down a different aisle, giving me the privacy to check my account and make sure the money had been credited back. But my balance was much lower than I expected and the bet was showing as settled, meaning the game must be over. *That's not right*, I thought. *There must be a mistake*. I was shaking as the result of the match downloaded. Azarenka had picked up an injury in the second set and retired, forfeiting the match. Because a set had been completed, the result stood with no refunds.

"Look, I've found them!" Emma appeared holding two toilet brushes. "Which one, do you think? This one's more expensive, but I think it'll last longer."

"You choose." I felt dizzy and needed to sit down quickly. I could have bought 8,500 toilet brushes for the amount I had just lost.

My stomach was churning. Inside, I was shocked, devastated. I felt as though I had just been mugged, but on the outside I had to appear calm. It was something I was used to doing. Over the last year I had learned to hide my emotions, win or lose; to bury my feelings, to block out my conscience and blunt my instincts. I was also taking decisions based on my gambling habits and not for any other logical reason. I had turned into a selfish, self-centred, cruel person who lacked a sense of humour and any feeling for anyone other than myself. There in Homebase, I realized I had become a different person, unrecognizable from the one I had been twelve months ago. I didn't like the new me.

"Come on, let's just buy the bloody thing. I have to get back for a very important call," I said.

Within two weeks I was searching the internet for credit again. I had lost everything I had won and emptied my bank account once more. But at least we had clean toilets.

One cold and dull month the madness that gripped me reached a new level. It was a Sunday and, as usual, we had eaten a fantastic Sunday lunch prepared by Emma's father. It should have been a family time, a time of relaxation and play. But I was worried. There was no money in my account and payday was two weeks away, so I made an excuse and drove back to the house, leaving Emma and the boys at her parents' house. I drove quickly while I considered my next step. I needed money fast and there was only one place to turn. I had at least an hour on my computer before Emma would be back with the boys.

"The payments are how much? What's the APR on that? You must be joking! No way! Goodbye." Surely I had stumbled on an illegal loan company. How could anyone charge 4,000 per cent annual interest? Then I found one that seemed to be offering a much more realistic rate of interest. It didn't take long to enter my details; the applications were very simple. I pressed the "Submit" button for an instant decision. A telephone number appeared on the screen, inviting me to call. I didn't care that it was a premium-rate number.

"What do you mean, I need a guarantor? I don't want you to write to anyone. Thanks and goodbye." But before I could hang up, they explained they did have a partner company that could help. The interest rate would be higher, but I could spread the repayments over twelve months and the money would be in my account that day.

Half an hour later the money was in my account. What I didn't realize was that I had called a loan broker. I thought I was calling the finance company direct, but instead I had called a company who charged me simply for searching for my loan and then placing it with a finance company. I could have done that myself, but now they had my card details and I realized, too late, that they could take further payments at a later date.

I'd stumbled headlong into the murky world of online loans.

In stark contrast to the highly regulated insurance industry with which I was so familiar, this world felt threatening and dangerous. Even then, it seemed to me that it was preying on people who were desperate for credit and perhaps those who lacked the knowledge to make a really informed decision. People like me? Or perhaps people less foolish, but just less fortunate than me.

The money arrived. As soon as I placed a bet on a late-afternoon football match, all my concerns about the stupidity of accepting the loan evaporated.

There was still half an hour until kick-off. Emma called to say she was staying at her parents' for tea. I had time and now I had money; I decided to experiment. I was receiving an increasing number of invitations to join the casino on my betting account.

I had only ever betted through the sports exchanges, but now I found myself considering an offer of a free bet on the tables.

I knew little or nothing about roulette or blackjack. Just before I met Emma, my brother and I had been skiing at Lake Tahoe, one of the top ski resorts in the Californian Rockies. After a day spent wine tasting in the Nappa Valley, we visited a casino across the border in Reno, Nevada. I didn't understand how to play anything, so I kept my money in my pocket. Duncan, on the other hand, seemed to know what he was doing at the roulette table and as his pile of chips grew, the waitresses brought more and more drinks. At about 3 a.m. I was ready to drop, so he cashed in his money and we left.

I could remember the rules vaguely, and decided to place a small bet on red. I didn't see it as money any more. Online betting rarely feels like spending money. You make a deposit from your card to credit your account. When you visit the casino, you exchange the value of your account for coloured chips. The remoteness of the currency makes the bet feel harmless. I guess it could be compared to buying a new bed. If you pay £300 for the bed online using a credit card, it feels less expensive than if you go to the shop and count out £300 in £5 notes. Online gambling, and the online casino in particular, suspends the reality of parting with real money. It *is* real money, though, and I tried to remind myself that I needed to keep money in my account to pay the bills until payday.

On the casino website, I was surprised to see a real and rather pretty lady with an Eastern European accent, welcoming new players and inviting us to place our bets. The little ball spun round with a satisfying hum and then it dropped with a "plunk". On a red number. I had just doubled my money in twenty seconds. All the adrenaline and excitement of betting on sports events seemed to be concentrated into this one spin of the wheel, even more intense than a horse race. I think I was hooked there and then.

The online casino caused the most serious destruction of all. This was the very height of my addiction. In a typical day I probably placed up to a thousand bets over a sixteen-hour period. A hardened drug addict probably only shoots up twice, maybe three times a day. There are only so many bottles of vodka an alcoholic can drink before they keel over. But a compulsive gambler can go without food or sleep until his account is empty. I was a fully paid-up member of the most expensive club in the world.

CHAPTER 25

Easy Credit

I hardly noticed as the gloomy spring turned into summer. Over the next six months I descended into a destructive pattern of behaviour that, deep down, I knew was going to end in a terrible and terminal way. I knew my marriage would probably end when Emma eventually found out we were broke. I also knew that my career was suffering; it was only a matter of time before they found out about my habit. But still I thought I could win all the money back.

All I needed was a winning run like the one I had enjoyed at the start of the year. I knew that time was running out, but that knowledge made me take even more risks than I would otherwise have done. I fell into the trap of easy but expensive credit. Once I had taken one loan, other loan options opened up.

I knew that, as a senior employee, my credit status was regularly checked at work. It was important that I kept up with my loan repayments. Many of the loans I took out were offered over a very short term. Each time I repaid them, I received an instant email or text of congratulations, inviting me to reapply, but this time with VIP status, meaning even faster payment and a higher credit limit. At the back of my mind, I knew what I was doing was madness, but I didn't accept I was a problem gambler in my conscious mind. I just thought I had been burned and was trying to put things right. It was just so easy to get credit and so easy to accept an offer of someone paying £600 into my account in minutes, with no paperwork to complete and very few questions asked. I knew I would need to find £800 to repay that loan in a month, but ever the optimist I convinced myself I could win enough to make the repayments. The reality was, I would lose the money and then have to take out another loan, or roll the loan over by paying the minimum monthly interest.

Very soon, I had created a debt spiral over which I had little or no control. I was plummeting downwards fast. But I still had to maintain a pretence of being in control. That meant lying to Emma about the reasons why we couldn't afford holidays or even some essentials. I lay awake each night thinking about what I had done, the life I had created. Although I was still gambling to try and win back money I now needed for essential everyday things, gambling had become something more than that. It was a place where I could escape the barrage of emails and calls from debt companies, a place where I could escape the reality of my life. Gambling was my medication, anaesthetic for the horrible reality of the life I had created.

It wasn't just online that I found credit. I visited high-street lenders offering high-interest, short-term loans. The application process was very simple. The first time I visited one of the shops, I waited in line behind two young men who had lost their jobs from the nearby headquarters of JCB. They were making their regular monthly payments and it was clear they had just received their benefit cheques. I felt bad. These were decent lads who had lost their jobs and were legitimately looking for money to live on. My motives were less honourable.

When my turn finally came, I was asked for a copy of my bank statement. My bank was opposite the shop so I crossed the road and requested a statement. I was genuinely horrified when it took several long minutes to print page after page. A queue had built up behind me.

"Sorry, I probably didn't explain. I just need the last thirty days," I said to the lady behind the counter.

"Yes, this is the last thirty days," she replied. When she finally handed it to me, it showed hundreds of gambling transactions.

I almost went straight back to the car. *They'll never give me a loan when they see this*, I thought. But I had long since lost any last drop of self-worth. Out of desperation for the money, I went back to the loan shop.

"Sorry, it's a bit long."

"It's OK. I just need to see evidence of your pay," the young girl replied.

I pointed it out. It was the only transaction in the credit column. When she went to the back of the shop to make a phone call, I was sure I would be declined. She wasn't on the phone for long.

"Your credit limit is £1,000. Is that OK? And you need to pay back £1,250 in thirty days. Just sign here while I count your cash."

As I said, quick and easy credit, even in the face of printed evidence that I was already in deep trouble.

One morning in early September, I woke with a strong sense of purpose. It was going to be a fine day. The sun was coming up, transforming the heavy dew that clung to the grass into millions of tiny diamonds. A very thin mist seemed to hover just above the surrounding fields so that trees emerged, spectre-like, standing to attention in the hedgerows. In another life, on a late-summer morning such as this, I might have asked Matthew if he wanted to hunt for field mushrooms with me. He would have sat high on my shoulders as we criss-crossed the fields, leaving patterns in the wet grass, just as I had done with my own father many years before. My childhood seemed an eternity away. But the days when I had time to take my own son off for an adventure also seemed like a lifetime ago. I had a long journey ahead of me. Yesterday I had made arrangements to meet Alex at his office in Wales.

After we shared pleasantries over the phone (which involved a great deal of lying on my part), I got down to business. "Listen, Al, I have to see a client in Bristol tomorrow. I know it's short notice, but can I swing by the office tomorrow, and we can have a proper catch-up? I haven't seen you in months."

"Of course you can. What time will you get here?" He sounded genuinely happy at the prospect. I suppressed a feeling of guilt. There was no client visit in Bristol and my motive for seeing him went way beyond our friendship.

I first met Alex when I was still in the Army; his wife and my first wife were close friends. We hit it off together straight away and found we had a huge amount in common, not least a love of rugby and skiing. Alex was brilliant with people and had an uncanny ability to see through anyone and understand what made them tick. He used this ability superbly in business. He had taken on a very senior role in the family company, a steel processing and wholesale firm, at a young age. The business was now flourishing and they had recently moved to a new site and invested in new machinery. Alex loved nothing more than showing me round the works every time I visited. As close to me as any brother, he had stood by me when my first marriage fell apart, even though this meant potential conflict with his wife. He was also a dutiful and diligent godfather – much more hands-on than I was as godfather to his eldest son.

I had enough money in my account to refill the petrol tank in the car. I set off early and arrived at lunchtime. I found Alex hard at work behind a huge computer screen. After bear hugs and a brief catch-up we donned our white hard hats and fluorescent vests and I followed Alex into the factory. He was obviously a popular boss and seemed to know all his staff by name. He was very proud of the shiny new machinery. Back in the office, we sat down over mugs of hot tea.

"What's on your mind, Justyn?" As ever, he'd seen through me and could sense I needed to ask something.

"I'm not sure how to say this, Alex. I've never asked you to help financially before, but – well, it's Matthew." I knew Alex loved his godson and would do anything he could to help. I was about to lie to my best friend in a terrible, calculating, heartless way.

"We've been told we should try and find out what happened to cause his stroke – whether there was any clinical negligence during the labour. We've found a lawyer to take this on, but we need to lodge a deposit with him. It's one of those no-win, no-fee cases, but we have to make a deposit up front." This wasn't all a lie. But the fact was, the lawyer who had agreed to take on the case had just secured legal aid. No deposit was needed.

"How much?"

"Five grand."

"When?" he asked me.

"Um... well, now, really. I could pay you back in about six months. I have a dividend payment due in January."

Alex didn't ask any questions. He wrote me a cheque there and then. I felt guilt as I drove away from the docks. Even when I told myself that the money would clear off all the payday loans, I still felt wretched. I had lied about something I knew Alex would respond to. It wasn't just a lie, it was betrayal. What kind of a friend was I?

I flicked on the radio. The sports bulletin followed the news headlines. Andy Murray was involved in a tight tennis match against Roger Federer; the final set was about to start. I dialled the familiar number and transferred £100 to my betting account and backed the Scotsman. All feelings of guilt disappeared as my heart beat faster. I found a radio station that was broadcasting the game and settled back in my seat. There was a tall lorry ahead of me going about fifty miles per hour. I drove up behind him and slowed the car to match his speed in his slipstream. I looked at the fuel gauge. If I was careful, I could make it home without refuelling.

CHAPTER 26

Terminal Velocity

It was three minutes to two on a cold, wet night. The damp north wind whipped through my dressing-gown, drenching me as I tried to shelter against the wall of the cottage in the lee of a howling gale. I cursed myself for not grabbing my coat and contemplated going back inside for it. A quick glance at my watch told me there was no time left and, in any case, I would run the risk of waking Emma. I pulled at my collar and huddled closer to the wall as I dialled the number of my bank. A quick automated check of my balance told me my salary had just been deposited. Good. Then I entered the number sequence that would take me through to the bank's call centre. It seemed to take forever. They probably didn't get many calls at this time of night.

"Good morning," I said when I finally got through. "I'd like to make a transfer between my accounts, please."

I was paid by automated transfer on the same day of each month and the money always hit my account at 2 a.m. The payday lenders knew this as well and they had my debit card details. They would always try and reclaim the full amount, but if they couldn't take it all, they took all they could. It was a mad rush for my money and I wanted to be at the front of the queue. I moved as much as I could into my savings account and then spent the following morning ringing up the lenders and apologizing for the lack of funds, reassuring them the money would follow shortly, and generally heading off unwanted phone calls and letters.

Once one of my lenders called the home number while I was at work in London. They wouldn't tell Emma what the call was about, but they left the name of the company. Emma, sharp as a whistle, Googled the name and called me to ask why a "short-term lender" wanted to talk to me. I quickly made some excuse that it was work-related, but I know she didn't believe me. She knew money was in short supply, but she had no idea why. I had just sold my car and made up yet another lie that it had come to the end of its lease. That evening we had another blazing row. I made some excuse that my payment structure had been changed and I was now paid on commission in retrospect and that there would be a lag in my pay. There were so many lies, I lost sight of what was real and what was pure fantasy.

Almost all my money was now disappearing to service my debt and pay for groceries and essential bills. I let the rent slip, but luckily the landlord had either not noticed, or was being incredibly nice by not chasing me. In order to feed my gambling habit, I looked elsewhere for credit. When I had taken out as many payday loans as I could, I called my mother and arranged to see her.

Like Alex, she was so pleased to see me. Her home in Kent was a long way from Derbyshire and my visits had become less frequent. I think she was a little worried about signing the guarantor loan documents when I laid them out before her, but I assured her that I had an excellent opportunity to buy more shares in the company and that I would repay her long before the term of the loan ended. As I worked in financial services, she trusted me, even though she didn't really understand what she was signing. Again, I felt guilt at the depths I could stoop to. If I missed a payment, the loan company would call Mum demanding money, and her own credit history would be affected. The loan was guaranteed against her house; I was risking something that wasn't even mine and lying about it. My wage was many times greater than my mother's. I completely abused the love she had for me and her trust in my judgment.

As usual, I sought and found escape from the horrible reality of what I had become by gambling. To fill the empty times between sporting events where there was nothing to bet on, I became frequent visitor to the casino. Soon, the thrill of the roulette table was so strong, it meant that my sporting bets were no longer enough to numb my feeling of self-loathing. Only the casino could now block my darkest thoughts.

Unlike the sports exchanges, you could bet on the casino round the clock. Oscar frequently woke in the night, and I always volunteered to sit with him as he fell back to sleep. I was being neither a loving husband nor a caring father; it was simply an opportunity to play roulette in the middle of the night while I bounced Oscar to sleep. This almost backfired on me once when I was watching TV with Emma, the boys and Emma's parents. A film was on and when a roulette wheel was shown during a break, advertising an online casino, Oscar pointed at the screen and shouted at the top of his lungs, "Look, Mummy, it's Daddy's work!"

And then, one Sunday, I did something that will haunt me for the rest of my life. We had just enjoyed our regular Sunday roast with Emma's parents. It could have been relaxing, but Matthew was desperate for me to take him to the swings. It was pouring with rain, but as an autistic child, once Matthew had set his mind on something, no amount of rationalizing would dissuade him. After an hour of his begging, I gave in. It was quite rare that just the two of us spent time together and I was actually quite looking forward to seeing the joy and laughter on his face as I pushed him on the swing or helped him climb the slide.

"You'll have to go back home for his coat; I left it on the peg this morning," Emma called to me as I lifted Matthew into her car. Matthew knew the way to the swings and he was very excited. He shouted loudly when he realized I wasn't driving directly there.

"I have to get your coat from the house first, little chap. It won't take long. I promise to push you higher than the hedge."

"No, Daddy. You have to push me higher than the sky!" His little eyes sparkled with anticipation.

I pulled up outside the house and left the engine running. As I unlocked the door, I could hear Matty calling, "Run, Daddy, run!" I grabbed his coat and then remembered a bet I'd placed that morning on an Indian premier league cricket match. One check of my watch told me it would be finished. I ran up the stairs and pressed the power button on the computer.

My balance indicated I'd backed the wrong team. I was cross. I had really been looking forward to spending time with Matty, and now it was all spoiled by bad feeling. I walked over to the window. I could see Matty; he was safely strapped in. He could wait a few more minutes while I placed a quick bet on red at the casino. Over the course of the next two and a half hours, I steadily emptied my bank account. When I had nothing left to lose, at least in my bank account, I slowly walked downstairs, feeling the enormity of what I had done.

Matty's eyes were closed and puffy. I could see the dried tear-streaks on his rosy cheeks where he'd cried himself to sleep.

As I drove back to Emma's parents' house in time for tea, I knew something had to give. I knew the crash had to happen soon. Perhaps I was willing it to happen, because what I did next was, I knew, so stupid and so irrational it could only lead to disaster.

CHAPTER 27

Crisis at Work

By the following weekend the fridge was empty, and we had no milk and no food for the coming week.

"We need to do a shop," Emma said as we sipped mugs of scalding black tea in the kitchen.

Emma had just taken a part-time job in the local pub. It was hard work and unsociable hours, but she knew we were short of money. I had no way of paying for the things we needed. I looked through my wallet, as though I might suddenly find a secret stash of £20 notes. The only card that still worked was the corporate card I used for work expenses. It looked very similar to one of my own credit cards. And then I remembered a story one of the directors had told me about a colleague who had accidentally used his corporate card to pay for shopping at a supermarket. There was no problem; the transaction was marked as a private expense and the money was deducted from source.

"Come on then," I said. "Let's go for a drive."

I pulled up at the garage and filled the car with petrol. The garage shop had a good selection of groceries and I piled our basket high. My card worked at the till. I reminded myself to declare the transaction and not claim it as a work expense. All through the week I kept expecting a phone call from the office asking me to explain the payment, but the call never came. I always intended to complete my monthly expense return, but somehow I just avoided it. I used the card again with increasing frequency. Each day when I woke, I expected a call from the office. I knew the call would come one day, but weeks turned into months. I still hadn't accounted for my expenses or paid any money back.

I needed cash urgently and found myself looking at the pictures hanging on the walls of our lounge with more interest than usual. In the days when I'd had plenty of money, I'd bought an original military cartoon by a famous artist. It matched a picture I'd been presented with when I left the Army. Now I found myself surfing the internet to try and establish how much they were worth. I was pleasantly surprised at their potential value. I still had the address of the dealer. He explained that demand had fallen, but he would be willing to give me half the amount I paid originally and quoted me a price for the pair. He was happy to pay cash if I could get to his gallery in Herefordshire, a four-hour round trip. I felt no remorse; I was just glad to have some cash.

In the weeks that followed I began to sell things I thought Emma wouldn't miss. My Breitling watch was one of the first things to go. It had been a Christmas present from Emma in the days when we were both earning. She immediately noticed it was missing. I told her I'd sent it away to be fixed under the guarantee. She didn't ask me why I wasn't wearing my wedding band for several weeks after I had sold it. The ring was unique and the inscription very personal and precious. The man who had examined it had been disappointed about the inscription on the inside of the gold band. It would have to be melted down. Perhaps Emma just didn't want to confront me, for fear of what I might tell her.

Years ago, on the day I met Emma for our first coffee date, I had noticed collection of military memorabilia at the antique shop in Ashbourne. Twice in recent weeks I had put my Sword of Honour in the car, intending to take it to be valued. Twice I had turned back. It was priceless; its value went way beyond the monetary. That sword represented all that was good about my life before I let gambling destroy it. I had saluted the Queen with it, and Harry and

I had used it in many games. It was the same sword he had used to make a one-sided arch outside the church on the day Emma and I were married. I had promised it to Harry, and had hoped that one day he would pass it down to my grandchildren and tell them about my achievements.

"It's difficult to value," said the dealer. "If you could write me a little paragraph about how you got it, that would help; then it has provenance." The sword had my name stencilled onto one side. My regimental crest and the date of my graduation in 1992 were marked on the other. "It could go for £200 or it could go for a lot more. You'd be better off selling it online to a specialist dealer."

"I want to sell it today; I'll probably change my mind if I take it home. Urgent tax bill to pay – you know how it is," I said.

"OK, I'll give you £200. Cheque OK?"

"No, cash please, if you can."

It had been so long since I had cried, but now I felt my eyes well up as I walked back to the car carrying the empty plastic bag. I choked back the tears. What had I just done? I felt as though I'd betrayed myself. I felt dirty and cheap. After I'd paid the money into my account, I rushed back to the online casino. It took just an hour to lose every penny.

One day, I went too far and in desperation sold a precious silver ornament, a gift to us from Emma's father. She noticed immediately. I told her I'd just taken it in for repair. Emma was furious with me this time. She had noticed how our possessions kept disappearing and now she wanted an explanation. I fled and found myself walking on the hills above the little village that had been home for the last two years. The grey clouds only just cleared the hilltop and a thin drizzle blew directly into my face. I could see no way out of the mess I had created. I surprised myself that I kept going each day. I felt very alone. I knew I'd caused all the trouble; now I was disgusted with myself and what I had become. I felt sorry for Emma and the boys. We had enjoyed such a privileged life until I had thrown it all away.

My lies were unsustainable. I knew the clock was ticking, both at work and at home. Each time I went to bed I pictured sand sliding quickly through an hour glass. It was the first thing I thought about when I woke. The only thin sliver of hope I held on to was that I might still strike it lucky with that big, elusive win. Then I could clear off my debts and repay my expenses at work. But deep down I knew that was very unlikely to happen.

On the Friday when the phone call finally came from my boss, I almost felt a sense of relief. It was late in June, the end of the first week of the Wimbledon Championships. My boss, trusting me, had assumed that the transactions were fraudulent, that my card had been cloned. He was almost apologetic at first. I told him the truth. We agreed to meet up on Tuesday, with the HR director. I watched dust particles dance in a ray of sunlight as I lay on the floor, still holding the phone long after I'd said goodbye.

Tuesday's meeting didn't take long. Over the weekend, they had looked at the emails in my account from the last few months and discovered that more than half the communications were from payday loan companies. It was quite clear I couldn't continue as an account director. We came to an agreement which avoided a disciplinary hearing. I had shares to cover the payments on my card. The whole thing was managed efficiently and sensitively. But I was now out of work, with little prospect of ever again working in the industry of which I had once been at the very pinnacle. There was no time to say goodbye to my friends and work colleagues.

But even the shock of losing my job didn't break my pride. I transferred the last of my money the day before the meeting and deluded myself that I would survive on my winnings. As I drove home from the office for the last time, I made a call. I should have called Emma and told her everything. Instead I called the telephone bet help desk and placed a £200 bet on a young Australian tennis player.

I wasn't at the bottom yet. I still had further to fall.

CHAPTER 28

Humiliation

It took me three weeks to tell Emma that I'd left my job for a better one. I truly thought I would walk into a new role very quickly. My skills were still in demand, even if I wasn't. I made some calls to old contacts and, after initial interest, the opportunities all seemed to end in the same cul-de-sac. It was a very small market and gossip was rife. No one wanted to take a chance on me at my level of entry and salary.

Alex was brilliant. As soon as he knew I'd lost my job he called to tell me he had arranged a meeting for me in London with the owner of the broking company he placed all his commercial insurances with. The owner lived on a Greek island, but Alex had persuaded him to fly back to London to meet me and talk about the possibility of me joining the company and starting a private client practice.

On the day of the meeting, I had the train fare in my account plus a little extra for lunch. I woke early to get ready. As I put my suit on, I convinced myself I could go without lunch. I logged on and put £10 on an even number. Within an hour, I had lost not only my lunch, but the money I needed for the train fare. Unable to think of any excuse that would be good enough for Alex, I simply turned my phone off. When he finally got through to me that evening, he was hopping mad. I lost my best friend that day. He had been my best man and I his. We were godfathers to each other's children. Our friendship had lasted through thick and thin; we had shared holidays together. He had always picked me up when I was down.

He had always been there for me. But that day was the end of our friendship. He hasn't spoken to me since.

About a month after I lost my job, we were staying at Emma's parents' for the weekend to make room in our own home for two of Emma's Cheltenham schoolfriends, with their partners and children. My office was being used for the weekend by one of Emma's oldest friends who now lived in Hong Kong with her husband, a solicitor. I was angry because I couldn't get to my computer. I resented them being there.

Both couples were lovely. Over the years, I had got to know the guys well on an annual golf trip to Portugal. Once, this trip had been one of the highlights of my year, but I had missed the last two years, making excuses about not being able to leave Matthew for the weekend.

I had intended to be in Jersey seeing Harry while these friends came to stay at our house, leaving Emma to stay with her parents. However, one of the worst things about losing my job was the end of my business trips to clients in Jersey, and the opportunity this afforded to visit Harry. Because it was expensive to get flights and even more expensive to find accommodation, I hadn't seen Harry for six weeks. My mother gave me the money for a flight and enough to pay for a hotel. I should have booked the flight as soon as the money came into my account. Instead, I let it sit there for two days. I couldn't stop thinking about it. I calculated that I just had time to use it to win a little more, so I could take Harry out for a meal and be able to transfer it back to my bank account in time to buy the plane ticket. I didn't win. I could hear the disappointment in Harry's voice when I told him I wouldn't be coming out to see him after all.

And so, here I was in Emma's parents' house, and I was angry. We were getting ready to drive back to our house to share the day with our guests when Emma took a call on her mobile. It was a short call.

"That was Niki. They've run out of hot water. Did you check the oil level like I asked?"

That was all I needed. The minimum delivery would cost me £500, and I still owed them for the last batch. They'd been chasing me for payment. I ripped into Emma, really losing my temper. She had done nothing wrong, though, and I soon felt guilty for taking my stress out on her. I checked the oil level as soon as we arrived at the cottage. There was a little left. Not much, but enough. They'd just used up all the hot water. Niki acted quite strangely when I told her. She blanked me for the rest of the day. I couldn't understand why.

That night I discovered the reason. It was earth-shattering.

I'd always been careful about covering my tracks. But that weekend, I hadn't tidied my desk very well. Niki saw a bank statement while she'd been putting on her makeup. She showed her husband and neither of them could believe what they saw. Now the truth was finally out, and in a very public way. Emma confronted me. She hardly dared ask me about the money she thought was locked away in a three-month bond. But now was a time for truth. There was nothing left to hide.

Emma was shocked, hurt and disgusted. I told her everything and held nothing back. Except for one thing. I just couldn't bring myself to tell her about the reason I lost my job. I had lied to her for so long, I'd forgotten how to tell the truth.

Emma moved back to her parents' house with Matty and Oscar, leaving me to stew. I felt terribly low, but also somehow liberated. One of the key things that had kept me gambling was the deluded belief that the only way to make things better was to win everything back before Emma found out. Now that didn't matter any more.

After a few days Emma came back to the house. The boys were missing me. They couldn't understand why they couldn't be in their house, and they wanted their daddy. Emma couldn't bring herself to look me in the eye. She was in shock and coming to terms with the fact that all her dreams were smashed and that I wasn't the man she had thought she had been living with.

I did some things I should have done years before, like closing my gambling account and excluding myself from opening another account with the online provider. Self-exclusion is a very simple and effective way of putting a "block" in place for problem gamblers. I called a gambling awareness helpline and fixed up one-to-one counselling sessions. At first Emma stood by me. She even drove me to Nottingham for counselling. She showed me there was hope; consequently, I didn't gamble. I thought the only reason I had carried on gambling for so long was to win back my losses before Emma found out, to make it right before she discovered all our money was gone. Now she knew, I thought I would just be able to stop gambling, since my reason to keep betting had disappeared. For that reason, I stopped going to the counselling sessions. It was a two-hour round trip and, although the sessions were free, the parking wasn't. Childcare was also a problem while Emma took me. If my sole reason for gambling was gone, surely there was no need to keep attending the sessions?

As the summer dragged on I tried to find a job, but always the same thing happened. I got to the stage where they needed references and then they made excuses or just didn't return my calls. As I faced up to the reality of the situation, I felt myself slipping into a deep depression. Without the gambling, I began to drink to anaesthetize the pain instead. I considered working part time as a gardener, but then realized I could live off benefits while I kept searching for a real, better-paid job. I had absolutely no self-respect, but I was still too proud to look for recovery.

One night towards the end of that summer I drank myself to sleep on the sofa. I awoke in the morning fully clothed, my head feeling groggy, and my body stiff and aching. The house was quiet when it should have been filled with laughter and the sound of Matty and Oscar charging about madly. Emma had gone. I knew she wasn't coming back.

My stupid pride prevented me from calling my wife. Instead, I wandered through the house. I found a few pounds in Matthew's piggy bank. After a long search, I found a £10 note in one of Emma's old handbags. I remembered the happy look on her face when I had given her that bag for Christmas. A lifetime ago. Upstairs I lay on the bed: *our* bed, a wedding present from my mother. The boys used to love bouncing on the bed, or making a cave to hide from me, a grizzly bear or a dragon, who would tickle them if they woke me from my pretend hibernation. Rolling onto Emma's side of the bed, I could smell her perfume. Then I saw her rings. The engagement ring I had given her on top of a beautiful snowy mountain; me on one knee, Emma laughing with embarrassment and joy. The wedding band I had placed on her finger on the happiest day of my life. She had stopped wearing the rings on the day she discovered my terrible secret. Now I was cross that she had abandoned me. I felt justified as I picked up both the rings, put them in my pocket and called a taxi.

Two hours later I was sitting at my desk, looking at all the different gambling sites offering me free bets and matched deposits. I had managed to sell Emma's rings for only a fraction of what they were worth, but I convinced myself I would win back the difference as I found an online casino. I took a sip of cheap wine and felt an old, familiar feeling of excitement wash over me.

The next morning I woke with an overwhelming feeling of guilt. I felt I had violated our marriage by selling the rings. Now that the money was gone and I had sobered up, I felt so low that I allowed myself to consider what it would be like to end my life. Would the boys be better off without me? Would it free Emma to move on with her life?

The next few weeks were the darkest of my life. I found a shop that would buy pretty much anything for cash. I sold Harry's game console and all his computer games. I sold wedding presents that were irreplaceable. I sold the boys' christening silver and furniture that had been in either my family or Emma's for generations. I found that I could get a few pounds for a bag of clothes. I was self-destructing. In my dreams I was hallucinating. I woke believing I was being chased. It felt as if I was being oppressed by a deep, malevolent evil. I wasn't eating. The house was a mess and I only came alive when I had a few pounds to bet with. I placed the most ludicrous ten- or twelve-leg accumulator bets and fantasized about the huge amounts I would win. I feel certain I was heading for the grave, or at least a stretch behind bars.

And then my mother, my father and my brother arrived. It was the day of my greatest humiliation; the day my pride was finally broken and my recovery began.

CHAPTER 29

CHAPTER 29

Train Crash

The day my runaway train finally came off the tracks was a Sunday. I knew it was Sunday, not because I did anything differently, but because the golf was on. I had persuaded one of the online betting companies to give me a "free" £10 bet, and I was just preparing to settle down to the commentary. I liked golf because it took all day to play the final round. I had plenty of time now, and golf allowed me longer to kid myself I could win.

I was rummaging around in the cupboards to see if I had anything to eat other than potatoes, when I heard a car pulling up outside and then another one. There was a knock at the door before I had time to see who had arrived. Should I hide? Would they go away? I opened the door. It was my brother and my mum and dad.

Mum was crying. She couldn't look me in the eye. Mind you, I couldn't take my eyes off the floor. We all went through to the lounge. One of Matthew's favourite wooden puzzles was still scattered on the sofa: I hadn't cleared it away since the day they left. I made space for them all to sit down and took a seat opposite them. I fixed my eyes on a picture hook on the wall above my dad's head. Until a few months ago, a valuable print had hung there, a present to myself when I was awarded a bonus at work. I had sold it for less than a quarter of its purchase price.

"We just want you to know we care about you. We don't have a plan. But we want to help you, in any way we can." Dad took the lead. He held up a piece of paper. There was nothing on it. "This is what we have, a blank page. You fill it, any way you want. It's your choice. We can find you some care. There are courses, residential courses. They cost money and there aren't many places, but if that's what you want…" He passed me the paper.

I felt like a schoolchild again. I knew it had to end, but it was going to end my way, not like this.

Mum had stopped crying now. "Or you could just come back with one of us. Today… now. You'll be safe. You can get help from there." She didn't plead with me.

This was humiliating. I felt like a sick child but I was a grown man. "Look, I really appreciate you making the journey up here," I said, "but I just need some time. Time to pack, to get my things together. Can I have a few days?"

There was a pause that seemed to take an eternity. They looked at each other and I felt excluded, as though I were a patient awaiting a terminal diagnosis and the doctors were considering how much to tell me. I looked down at the floor and noticed for the first time that day that my socks were odd and my toes were sticking out of holes on both feet.

It was Duncan who broke the silence. He had kept quiet up to that point. Taller than me, with the intimidating physique of a rugby player, my younger brother is genuine and always direct. He stood up. "Come on, Justyn; let's get some fresh air."

It was a sunny day in late October. One of those still, clear days that follow a storm, when the wind has battered the trees and stripped them of their golden-yellow foliage overnight. Now the last of the leaves danced in the bright light as they tumbled to the ground. I had always enjoyed autumn: the clarity of the light, the colour of the hedgerows and trees as they turn from dark green to brown and gold. I loved the way the countryside settled down for a rest after producing its fruit. This year, I hadn't noticed the transformation of the leaves, or even the change in season. The brightness of the low sun in the bright blue sky hurt my eyes. I felt as if I was emerging from a dark cave after months of hibernation.

Duncan was blunt, honest and brutal. Just what I needed. "Tomorrow at 10 a.m., a removal van is coming to pack up the house. The lease runs out on Wednesday. The rent has been paid up by your father-in-law. He's helping to pack up tomorrow and he doesn't want to see you. We are leaving today and you need to come with us."

I realized I had two options. I could go home with my mum, tail between my legs, back to the room I left twenty-five years ago. Or I could walk the streets for the winter.

As we headed back to the house, I started to cry uncontrollably. I hadn't cried like that for thirty years, since the night my dad came into my bedroom and told me Mum was about to die. I was thirteen years old then. I didn't lose my mum, but I lost the ability to really cry, until now. I was howling as I gave my mum and dad a hug. Between sobs, I thanked them for coming. I told them I was sorry: sorry that I had let them down; sorry that I had caused so much pain. "You've been so kind and I've been such a fool. I'm ready. I want to go home now."

They didn't say anything; they just smiled at me. Inside I felt raw humiliation as all the walls I had built around me came tumbling down in a heap.

"Let me put some things together. I'd like to say goodbye to Emma."

I called her and asked her to come over. "I'm going back with Mum. Can you bring the boys over?" I asked her.

"I think it would just confuse Matty. But I'll drive over now." There was no warmth in her voice.

I walked with Emma along the country lane where we used to push Oscar in his pram, while Matty had sat on my shoulders or jumped in muddy puddles. Walking towards Distant Point and a life that could have been, I remembered days filled with laughter and Emma's smile that lit up her face and could take away all my doubts and fears. Now the lane seemed empty. The huge gulf between us was wider than the Grand Canyon. We passed the little bridge where the boys loved to play Pooh sticks, and our "favourite bench" where we used to sit and make up stories. It was important to me that Emma knew I still loved her, despite the fact that I had allowed an addiction to take over my life, draining me of my emotions, my happiness and my spirit.

"Maybe one day you'll be able to forgive me. Look after the boys, please. I wish you'd let me say goodbye to them."

"Matty's confused enough anyway. He keeps asking where you are, why we don't live in our house any more. He has autism, for God's sake. Did you think he would just come up and give you a cuddle, then wave you off into the sunset? And Oscar's not even three years old yet. He can't work out why you don't read to him at night or tuck him up any more. Get real!"

I was crushed and teary. Hit by the enormity of what I had done, my sense of loss was profound. By continuing to gamble I had been able to avoid facing the reality of this moment, postponing the inevitable crash that was now happening around me. It was horrible – the more so because I knew it was entirely self-inflicted. This was all my fault.

I wanted to reach out and touch Emma, but the fear of rejection held me back. She walked with her arms folded tightly across her chest. Every time I stepped close, she took a step away. Her eyes were cold, her lips set tight. *She's not going to hug me or tell me it's all going to be OK*, I thought. But I wished she would at least tell me the boys still loved me. Instead she was cold and distant. I had hurt her more than anyone had ever hurt her before. I had betrayed her and lied to her and stolen not only her money, but also her dreams and her smile. She drove off and I felt lost and alone, hopeless and broken.

It was starting to get dark. Dad had left and my mum was keen to start the long journey back to Kent. I found a bin liner and quickly went from room to room gathering what possessions I had left. My humiliation was complete as Duncan watched with an expression of concern mixed with pity. I had once been his hero. I had rescued him from the school bully, taught him to swim and fish. He had looked up to me as I left home, went to university and then on to the Army.

My mum stood with Duncan. She had been there to see me winning sports day cups and swimming competitions up and down the country. She had been in the crowd as I was presented with the Sword of Honour at Sandhurst. Now she watched as I grabbed my last few possessions. In the lounge I picked up a photograph of the house where Matty had been born: the Victorian townhouse with views across the picturesque market town of Ashbourne; the house we had sold at a profit, all of which I had squandered. Until recently, that picture had been encased in a silver photo frame, a wedding present. I had sold the frame.

I took one last look at the boys' toys. There were the tractors, cars and lorries Matty loved lining up in long, snaking traffic jams. There too were the board games he begged me to play each morning. Still more tears fell as I slowly closed the door. The walls of the old cottage were quite thick, leaving deep windowsills that were excellent for displaying the more precious items we once owned. It was here that I had kept the Sword of Honour. Now, still quite clear in the last of the fading light, was the dusty outline where the sword had once been on display.

In my office upstairs, I found more pictures, an old diary and a pair of cheap cufflinks. There were a few framed certificates above the desk. One recognized my achievement in my insurance exams, another was an award for winning the company's biggest client in the UK. I had no need for either of them now.

I dumped the huge pile of unopened mail – letters from angry creditors and debt-collection companies, and domestic bills – into my bin liner. I pulled open a drawer in the desk. I still had a set of satellite navigation disks for the Porsche Cayenne I used to drive. In another life.

I didn't really know when I would next see the boys, so I spent my last few minutes saying goodbye to them privately. I'd been avoiding their bedrooms ever since they left. Their beds were still unmade from the last night they had slept in them. As I flicked on their bedside lights, the emotion almost choked me. In Oscar's room the enormity of my loss hit me again. I fell to my knees, clutching the soft blanket I used to tuck him in with. I will never forget the smell of that blanket. It was the smell of a loss that was almost too much to bear.

It was no easier in Matthew's room. He loved books and there was a large bookcase on the left side of the room. Every book held a reminder of a happy bedtime. I kissed his pillow, my tears leaving wet marks on the cotton covers. Turning my back on the little bedroom, I walked away.

It was a long journey back to Kent.

PART 5

Twelve Steps to Recovery

A **twelve-step program** *is a set of guiding principles (accepted by members as "spiritual principles") outlining a course of action for recovery from addiction, compulsion, or other behavioral problems.*

WIKIPEDIA

CHAPTER 30

Step 1

We admitted we were powerless over our addiction – that our lives had become unmanageable

Dawn. One by one, my senses slowly returned. I heard birds singing. I could smell coffee. Dull, grey light peeped through a gap in the curtain as my eyes struggled to open, allowing me to recognize the safe familiarity of a room I had called my own twenty-four years ago. How impatient I had been then for the adventure of adulthood, how excited by the prospect of leaving home to make my fortune in the big world. The black bin liner on the floor next to the desk where I had studied for hours was all I had left. In it was the fortune I had made: a few old clothes, photos of people I loved but had let down, and a pile of letters demanding money I didn't have. I rolled over and found sleep once more.

There was a knock at the door. My mother put the tray on the desk: a mug of coffee and a plate of hot buttered toast. I felt like a teenager again. I couldn't stop saying thank you, over and over.

"Andrew will be here in half an hour. I just spoke to him on the phone and he wants to talk to you."

"Who's Andrew?" I asked.

"He's my financial adviser. He said he could help with your debts."

"Oh, thank you…" My favourite words.

It wasn't difficult talking to a complete stranger. Andrew was friendly and understanding. Not only was he Mum's financial advisor, but he was a friend from her church. The smile on his grey-bearded face was natural. So too was the look of concern in his eyes as I explained my situation.

"We need to get you to WKDA – West Kent Debt Advice. They can help you. They're an independent charitable organization, and they don't charge. I'll see if I can get you an appointment this week. Their office is at our church."

I was touched by the genuine and sincere care he had for me.

"Here's my card. Please call if you need me. I'll let you know when I've fixed an appointment for you."

I shook his hand and thanked him for the tenth time. My overwhelming feeling that first day was a sense of security. I felt protected. It reminded me of a time when I had broken my ribs playing rugby and ended up having to stay in hospital for five days due to some internal bleeding. The pain was still there, but I felt confident that the nurses who fussed round me and delivered the pain-numbing medication would fix me, and that it would be only a matter of time before I was well enough to go home.

I am so grateful to my mother for not lecturing me or asking me about what happened. She just welcomed me home and let me go at my own pace. She showed me love in practical ways. It didn't feel like a dramatic new beginning, or even as though I was starting out on a new path. More like I'd just completed a very long journey and now I was wandering home, where a hot bath, food and a warm bed were waiting for me.

I slept a lot that first day and I did something I'd not done in a long time. I got down on my knees and I prayed. I asked God to forgive me for all the lies, the deceit, the stealing, the hurt and pain I had inflicted on the people I loved the most. I knew I had become a shadow of the person I once was and asked God to mend my broken life and try to make me whole again. And I made a promise to Him, that if He could mend me, I would live my life in the way it was intended; I wouldn't be selfish or full of my own importance. I didn't experience a flashing light, or feel a sudden surge of electricity, but I became aware of the reality of my life. I understood what I had done and I felt the hurt I had caused so many people. It was perhaps the same as for Ebenezer Scrooge in Charles Dickens' *A Christmas Carol*, when he was shown the truth of his past and the reality of the present. It changed him fundamentally and he suddenly had a new set of priorities in his life. That's exactly how I felt as I knelt quietly in my room. I had no idea what the future held, but I was determined to be honest and open about what I had done and not try to hide anything. I knew that the consequences and fallout from my behaviour would be massive, but I was ready to face up to it.

That evening in early November 2012, Duncan drove me to a Gamblers Anonymous meeting. I was feeling nervous about the evening; I would probably have run away if Duncan hadn't been there to take me in. But as soon as I walked in through the doors of the old church hall, I knew it was a good decision. I was greeted by someone my age. He looked completely normal. He gave me a little orange book which contained something called "The Twelve-Step Recovery Programme". I later learned this is a series of spiritual principles designed by two Christian men in America in the 1930s. Thousands of people have found recovery from compulsive behaviour since then by following the steps.

Here, in this room, were others in the same situation as me, people who understood. They didn't try to give me any advice; they just shared their own experiences. I felt very emotional and came close to tears several times as I listened to tragic story after tragic story. I took heart as people spoke of their own recovery and their hopes for a better future without gambling. The meeting lasted two hours, but it seemed to flash by. With five minutes left, I'd managed not to cry. Until the person on my right told us all how his wife had just left with his young children as a result of his gambling, and how he had to explain to his five-year-old son why he no longer lived with him. I wiped at my tears, determined not to let this room full of grown men see me cry. And then they asked me if I would tell them my story. I tried, but I broke down in tears so many times, I'm not sure how much they actually heard. At the end of the meeting I was stunned by their response. People I had never spoken to before came over and hugged me. They told me that it would get better, that I wasn't on my own, that they shared the same feelings that churned inside me. I promised I would come back the following week. I haven't missed many Monday evenings since.

Alone in my bedroom, I rummaged about in my black bin liner and found what I was looking for. As I opened my Bible something fell to the floor. I picked it up and recognized the initials "J" and "E" intertwined at the top of the scrap of paper. On the note, in Emma's beautiful handwriting, was "Numbers 6:24–26". These verses had been read at the very end of our wedding service. I found hope as I read them. I closed my eyes and realized it was the first day in two years I hadn't placed a bet. I was asleep in seconds.

I'm sure I would have slept through the night, but my phone rang just before midnight.

"Am I speaking to Justyn Larcombe?" the voice on the line asked. She sounded businesslike. I thought the accent might be South African.

"Yes, that's me," I said, my head groggy with sleep.

"I'm Tracy, calling from MHB. You have a balance of £1,174.27 outstanding on the loan you took out with us. You haven't kept up with the repayment schedule we agreed with you back in September. Interest is being charged daily on the account balance. I can take a debit card payment from you now for the full amount."

"I can't make a payment. I lost my job in June and I don't have any income right now," I explained.

"How much can you pay now?" she asked without the slightest hint of sympathy.

"I don't have anything I can pay. I told you, I have—" I didn't get the chance to explain further.

"I can take a holding payment and then we can reschedule the future payments. You must have £10 we can take. Do you still have the same debit card details we have on file?"

"I don't even have a pound right now. Look, can we talk tomorrow? I have no job, I just lost my house, and my wife left with the children. This is the third time you guys have called me today and it's the middle of the night, for God's sake!"

"If you aren't working you should have a P45 form, yaa? We need to see your P45. If you scan it to me and ring me tomorrow with a payment, we can reschedule. Is there someone who can give you some money – maybe a family member, yaa? Or we'll have to send someone round to discuss it, maybe instruct the bailiffs. OK?"

They could send anyone they wanted; there would be nothing there at the house to take. Thoughts of the cottage brought back memories of the boys. It took longer to get back to sleep this time. My pillow was wet when I finally drifted off.

CHAPTER 31

Step 2

We came to believe that a power greater than ourselves could restore us to a normal way of thinking and living

David was the full-time leader of West Kent Debt Advice. I quickly realized he was a no-nonsense man. He talked straight and expected the same in return. I could imagine him negotiating with Tracy from MHB, not giving an inch. We went through every debt, including anything I owed to friends or family, and calculated a figure. I was shocked that it had climbed to more than £70,000. I was no longer claiming and didn't want to claim any benefits and I did have some income. I was still helping with insurance exams and marking papers on a consultancy basis, so there was some money coming in – not much, but enough to make a sensible repayment offer.

"With the information you've just given us, we can create your financial statement. This is a really powerful document; it shows the creditors what you need to live on and what you can afford to pay them. It helps me to negotiate on your behalf and get them to freeze the interest so the situation doesn't get any worse." I got the feeling David was looking forward to doing battle on my behalf.

As I left the church building I felt a huge sense of relief. I felt as though I'd been fighting against a big army all on my own with my bare hands, and now the cavalry had just arrived, armed to the teeth with the latest weapons. David agreed to allow his office to act as a postbox, so all my mail would come to the church and not to my mum's house. I was told to refer all the phone calls to him.

I made it known that I had more time to take on a few more projects relating to exams. But I needed my computer for this work. That would mean I had access to the internet. So far I hadn't betted, but the temptation might be too great if I had access to around two and a half thousand online betting sites. It would be impossible to self-exclude myself from them all, and the very act might mean facing additional temptations.

I discovered the solution one Monday evening at a Gamblers Anonymous meeting. The meetings provided support, friendship and understanding, but they didn't directly offer any practical advice, other than the anecdotal "therapies" we took it in turns to give. All kinds of people attended the meetings – male and female, the old and the young. I discovered that problem gambling affected people from all parts of the social spectrum. There were those who couldn't drive past a motorway service station without stopping for a few hours to play the fruit machines; there were older folk who had retired and sold the businesses they'd spent their lives building up, only to lose everything after they took up gambling because they were bored. There were those who spent their days in gambling shops and those addicted to casinos. There were women who couldn't stop playing bingo and men who, like me, hid their online habits from their wives. I heard stories of broken families, suicides and people who'd been sent to prison because of their gambling. But I also heard stories of hope from people who had found recovery. I loved to hear these stories the most. I listened intently to every word these people spoke, to try and pick up on any words of wisdom, any tips they had to offer.

I quickly discovered that putting "blocks" in place was really effective in preventing slips or relapses. For many, this meant giving up their access to money and letting their wives control the finances.

"If I was an alcoholic, I wouldn't walk about with a can of Strongbow in my pocket. It's the same thing with my money. I don't need forty quid in my wallet each day. A couple of pounds for a sandwich is all I need – the missus keeps the rest."

This might have worked for me, but it was too late to ask Emma to manage my finances. Thanks to me, she was struggling to manage her own. Cash in my wallet had not been too much of a problem for me, as I never went to the high-street bookies to bet. But then my ears pricked up when I heard that someone had shared my compulsion for online gambling.

"I installed some software – it only cost £20 or something – but it blocks access to all the gambling websites. If I try and access something I shouldn't, it sends an email to my wife!" he said.

I liked the idea of that and the following day I installed some software called "K9". Mum agreed to act as the administrator. Of course, I could always have used a different computer. I knew there was one at the library. But this block on my home computer was the single most effective practical step I ever took to stop gambling.

I still had phone calls from creditors. The payday lenders were the most aggressive and showed no sympathy for my situation. At first all the creditors seemed angry that I had appointed a debt adviser. They told me it would have been better if I'd gone to them directly; they had their own advisers they could recommend who would be much cheaper. I told them I wasn't paying anything for advice and gradually they all stopped calling me. David wrote to me two weeks after my first appointment to say that all the creditors had agreed to accept a small affordable amount each month and none of them would charge me any interest.

After I read his letter, I went for a walk. It was a clear, frosty morning early in December and the sky was blue and cloudless. I walked through woods and across fields and felt free of the dark, oppressive clouds that had swallowed me up for the last two years. I kicked through a big pile of dry brown leaves and thought how much Matty and Oscar would love to do the same.

Step 2

I missed them enormously and wondered where they would be for Christmas.

When I got back to the house it was getting dark and the western sky was a watery pink. There was a car I didn't recognize parked in the driveway. Mum had been waiting for me and she met me in the hallway as I took off my boots. She had a huge smile on her face and held out a set of keys.

"It was Barby's. She can't drive any more. She wants you to have it so you can drive back home and see the boys." She handed me the car keys. I was speechless. Barby had been a close friend of Mum's for many years. The kindness people were showing me was overwhelming and totally undeserved.

I called Emma and asked her if I could come and see the boys. Emma was living in a small cottage not far from where we once lived. She felt safe there and it took a lot for her to even tell me the address, but she knew the boys would love to see me. I had no money for a hotel, so she kindly agreed to let me stay. She was working a late shift at the pub and had been invited to a party after work, so I could babysit. It seemed to work out well.

I pulled up outside the little terraced cottage that would once have housed a farm worker and his family. It was pouring with rain. I turned off the engine and listened to the steady drumming on the roof of my new car. Although I was desperate to see the boys, I took a moment before I braved the rain. Looking at the little house, I felt terrible that my behaviour meant my wife was now struggling to bring up two young boys, one of whom had special needs, on her own. She worked shifts in a pub to supplement the small amount of state benefit she was entitled to. This had definitely not been a part of our life plan when we first got married.

The boys were looking out for me and now their little faces were pressed against the glass of the front-room window as I ran down the path to Emma's front door. They jumped on me before I was even through the door. I opened my arms wide for them both and I will never forget that cuddle. Then there was a mad dash as they insisted on showing me around every room, cupboard and drawer in the whole house.

In contrast to the warmth and joy of the boys, Emma was cold and kept her distance from me. I think she still felt a deep loathing every time she looked at me. But I was determined to try and establish a relationship that would work in front of the boys. I had no reason to argue with her; she had been completely in the right and I had been in the wrong. How could I complain if she was angry with me?

I offered to take the boys to the swings and buy some food from the supermarket, but Emma was worried I might bump into her dad in town. It dawned on me then that I wasn't welcome in Derbyshire. Not only Emma's family, but all our old friends were very angry about what I'd done to Emma and the way I had treated her. She had told them the full facts. They knew I'd taken all her savings and they knew how I'd spent them. It shouldn't have come as a shock to discover that I was a hated man, but it did. I realized how naïve I had been to think I would be able to step straight back into my old life now that I wasn't gambling. The realization that the damage might be irreparable hit me like a punch to the stomach.

I loved putting the boys to bed that evening. I think I fell asleep as I read them the twentieth book. I woke the next morning and opened my eyes to see Matthew was smiling and staring at my face as he lay next to me. It was just before five and still very dark outside.

"I missed you, Daddy," he said, as he touched my nose to see if I was real.

"I missed you too. What shall we do today?" I whispered, not wanting to wake Oscar.

"Let's play 'Garage Is Open'! Because I love that. Yesterday, a long time ago, I always used to play that with you." Poor Matty always got his time jumbled up. I scooped him up and we tiptoed downstairs, pretending I was a chair-lift. He lined all his cars up for me and it was my job to put petrol in them. This was his favourite game and I felt a stab of pain as I thought of all the times he must have wanted to play with me, but I had not been there for him.

Oscar came down an hour later and wanted a cuddle on the sofa. It was still dark outside. The rain had cleared overnight, leaving clear skies and a very heavy frost. "Where's Mummy?" he asked.

"Probably sleeping in her bed."

"No, she isn't. I went to see her when I woke up. She must be in the bathroom."

Oscar was right. Emma's bed had not been slept in, but she wasn't in the bathroom either. I checked my phone to see if she'd left me a message. There were no missed calls and no texts. I dialled her number, but the call rang out. I pulled the curtain back in the lounge. Heavy frost glinted in the moonlight.

I began to feel worried. The route back from the pub was about seven miles of quiet country lane. What if the car had slipped off the road on the way home from the party and she was trapped, freezing somewhere in one of the many ditches? I rang the police and asked if there had been any accidents reported. They promised to ring me back. Half an hour passed and then it struck me that she may well have driven home to her parents' house – it was much closer to the pub. Perhaps, when she saw the icy conditions, she had been sensible enough not to risk the longer journey. I tried Emma's mobile once more before I rang her parents.

Her father answered. He was a little concerned too. There was no sign of Emma. He said he would drive the route.

It was still dark when the police car pulled up. The boys were excited to see a real police car. It filled me with nothing but dread. I was expecting the worst when I saw the serious expressions on the two officers' faces. I invited them in, my heart thumping in my chest.

"There's been no report of an accident overnight. I assume this is your house?" Both policemen were standing. The shorter of the two took notes while the other asked me the questions. It made me nervous.

"Um, no. This is my wife's house – we've been separated for a while. I just came up to be with the boys. I live in Kent." I was stammering, for the first time in my life.

"When exactly did you last see her and what time did you notice she was missing?" I felt a distinct change in their attitude towards me. It made me even more nervous. I felt guilty even though I had only been trying to help. Oscar came in and clung to my leg, shyly looking up at the uniformed policemen.

They were still questioning me when my phone rang. It was Emma.

"Hi, it's me," she said, her voice sounding very croaky.

"Oh, thank God," I said.

"What on earth is all the fuss about? My dad's just called me. He is so pissed with you. I didn't tell him you were staying here, and he's not happy about you waking him in the middle of the night. He wants to see you."

"I was worried about you. It's icy and I thought you might have crashed on the way home," I said weakly.

"If you were really worried about me you would never have behaved like you did. Well, it's too late now. I just had too much to drink, so I stayed at Laura's house, that's all. Now you've woken the whole house up here. It's not even seven."

I suddenly remembered the policemen, who were eyeing me intently. "It's OK, it's my wife. She's at a friend's house. I'm so sorry I troubled you."

"We need to speak to her, please, sir."

I passed them the phone.

"No, we'll need to ring her, if you don't mind," the tall one said.

When I explained to Emma she flew off the handle. "Why have you involved the police? I only went to a bloody party!"

The police left after calling Emma. I thanked them for coming, feeling even guiltier, ashamed that I had wasted their time.

Emma returned later that morning. She said her father was very cross and I needed to go and see him right away. Emma told me to say goodbye to the boys. There were tears and Matty clung to me tightly. In the end Emma had to pull him off my leg. I hated to leave them and I was dreading the confrontation ahead.

They say the love a father has for his daughter is a very tight bond. Emma, with three brothers, was David and Dorothy's only daughter, and the youngest of the four. We went through to the kitchen. This was the very room in which I had once asked permission to marry their daughter. For twenty minutes I listened as David shouted. I had no defence, I just took the blows and tried to say sorry. David told me he had fantasized about different ways to kill me. He described some of them to me. He wished it would be a long, slow and painful death. When he had run out of things to say, Dorothy took over where he left off.

"I can't believe you have the audacity to simply turn up and spend a night in Emma's house," she said.

This was the first thing they had said that wasn't actually fair or true, and I found myself defending my action, when I should have just accepted their anger.

"Sorry, but she said I could stay. I just wanted to be near the boys."

"Rubbish! She wouldn't let you back into her life. You must have found the address and just invited yourself in. That house was a safe place for her. How dare you just drop in like you own the place!"

I realized they didn't believe a word I was saying. Amazingly, this surprised me. It was only much later that I understood. Having pathologically lied about most things for the last two years, I couldn't expect people to believe anything I said now, or for at least the next two years to come. Something inside me flipped. I was in the wrong; I knew I was the cause of so much pain and hurt; but this just wasn't true – Emma must have let her parents think I'd shown up out of the blue. The weekend had been planned for several days. I lost my temper. Maybe that was what they had been waiting for; it gave them an excuse to throw me out.

I wrote them a long letter that week. I apologized unreservedly for everything. I made no excuses for my behaviour and I told them that I hoped one day they might forgive me. I didn't expect a reply and I didn't get one.

I had plenty of time to think as I drove back to Kent. The debts and the financial damage could be repaired. The relationships and trust would take longer. As I drove down the M1 in darkness, I recognized that perhaps these things, the things that were actually much more important than money, might never get fixed. I realized I had been kidding myself into believing I could just stop gambling and then walk straight back into my old life and carry on as if nothing had happened. I now knew that was certainly not the case. Someone much wiser than me had tried to explain what it was like trying to restore a relationship after it has broken down. She said it was like a garden. Once the garden had been well tended and full of flowers and colour and life. But the garden had been neglected and had become choked with weeds. The old garden was gone, and it would take time to restore it to its former glory.

I could have dwelt on my loss and felt sorry for myself, but every day I didn't gamble was a better day. My head was clear and I was thinking logically. I was also determined to make things right again.

CHAPTER 32

Step 3

We made a decision to turn our will and our lives over to the care of God

I was so excited as I placed the little star on top of the tree. Like many of the decorations I'd found in the box in Mum's attic, I recognized it from my childhood. Their association with the excitement and magic of childhood Christmases made me smile. Everything felt possible. I'd just been paid for marking almost 200 exam scripts and I wanted to make sure Emma and the boys had a Christmas to remember. Mum had been generous too and we spent the morning food shopping together for the feast I planned to cook on Christmas Day. That afternoon I had driven twenty miles to find a shop that sold Emma's favourite cheese. I spent several days hunting through crowded shops to find the right gifts. I didn't have much to spend, but I knew they would all like what I had chosen. Harry was flying in after Boxing Day. I was feeling happier than I'd felt in a long time.

A bottle of champagne was chilling in the fridge for Emma; Oscar's favourite DVD was ready by the television and Matthew's cars were lined up ready for a grand opening of the Daddy Garage! I glanced at my watch (£19.99 from a catalogue) for the umpteenth time and tried to picture where they might be on their journey down. I was determined to make this the best Christmas ever. Emma's parents were going away and Emma had agreed to bring the boys down for the holiday. She hadn't wanted to stay at first, but finally she agreed as long as she was free to see her friends in London after Christmas Day. I put another log on the fire and watched restlessly at the window.

When Emma's car drew up, I rushed out to greet them in the rain. Before they had even had a chance to unstrap their seatbelts I opened Emma's car door.

"Come on into the warm. I'll unload the car. There's some of your favourite fizz in the fridge. How was the journey?"

Poor Emma. I think my enthusiasm overwhelmed her, and she snapped back at me: "It was a horrendous journey, thanks. Sat in traffic on the M25 forever. Matthew needed a wee and Oscar spilt his drink all over himself before we were even on the motorway. I don't want any fizz. I've got a stinking cold, I just want to go to bed." She pushed past me and lifted the boot to take out the cases.

"Let me do that, please," I said.

"Just lift Matthew out, will you!" she shouted.

It would be fair to say that Christmas didn't quite work out the way I had intended. Emma really did have a streaming cold and was suffering, but I took her lack of participation in the Christmas celebration very personally, thinking she was deliberately trying not to enjoy herself. She didn't touch the cheese or drink the champagne; she just slept or stayed in her room. I thought she was trying to make a point that she wouldn't play happy families, but the reality was that she was feeling awful. I know that now, because I developed the cold after they all left. Which was lucky really; it meant I couldn't smell the cheese. I just couldn't bring myself to throw it out.

The house felt empty and quiet without them. It was cold and grey outside. As the old year ended and a new year began, the reality of my situation dawned on me. Over Christmas, Emma had explained that she was seeing a solicitor to talk about divorce.

Step 3

Early in January, the day after Harry flew back to Jersey, I packed all the Christmas decorations away in their box and lifted it back up the steps to the attic. There was no hiding the fact that I was feeling blue. I had little work and lots of debt. But I wasn't gambling and I hadn't had any urge to. There was a time when I would have looked to escape from unhappy feelings by placing a bet. I understood now that betting had been the place I ran to if I was bored, or sometimes the reward I gave myself if I felt happy. Although I didn't want to go to that place again, I hadn't yet found anything to replace it.

Mum's attic was cluttered with old furniture and neatly labelled boxes. With time to kill, I found myself exploring. I hadn't seen many of the things I found up there in twenty-five years or more. I began to feel quite nostalgic. One cardboard box was labelled "Justyn's things". It was dusty and mice had nibbled at the corners. I pulled it out from the eaves and untied the string.

In the box I found old school photographs, certificates and newspaper cuttings. But most of the space was taken up by my swimming medals. As I picked up the ribbons and read the inscriptions on the backs of the gold, silver and bronze medallions, I felt something stir inside me. It was a yearning, a feeling that I had some unfinished business. I had always felt my swimming career had ended prematurely, not cleanly and not even happily.

Later that evening I was sitting with Mum by the fire watching an old *Morse* DVD I'd seen several times. As the familiar, haunting signature tune signalled the end of the programme, I turned to Mum. "I think I might go for a swim in the morning, " I said.

Mum smiled. "OK. I'll be up early. What time will you go?"

"Probably just after six." I went to bed with a new sense of purpose.

CHAPTER 33

Step 4

We made a searching and fearless
moral inventory of ourselves

The next morning, the pool was surprisingly crowded. I chose the fast lane and felt as though I was trespassing. I got a few fierce looks from the serious swimmers, in their hats, goggles, racing trunks or smart Lycra swimsuits. My shorts were old and baggy. Still, it felt good to be exercising again and I held my own that first morning. I made the swim part of my daily routine. It wasn't long before I replaced my baggy shorts with a more modern pair, and within a few weeks I was racing up and down the pool, to even more fierce looks from the other swimmers.

One day I arrived early at the pool and had to wait outside the changing rooms. I walked over to the trophy cabinet. It was filled with cups and trophies belonging to my old swimming club. On the upper shelf were two very familiar photographs. The first was of a huge trophy, awarded to the club for winning the London League. The trophy was so large that it had to be held aloft by four swimmers; one of them was a seventeen-year-old me, looking very pleased with myself. The other picture was even older. It had inspired me as a teenager. Taken on a boat just after a successful Channel crossing, it showed eight swimmers from my old club, Royal Tunbridge Wells Monson, who had just set the record for the youngest team crossing of the English Channel. At an average age of 12 years and 130 days, it is a record which still stands to this day. The first time I looked at the picture, I wanted to swim the Channel. And now I felt that same surge of ambition.

Endurance or marathon swimming is very different from the type of competitive, short-distance swimming I was used to. Swimming the English Channel is recognized as the pinnacle of the sport and involves crossing the Dover Strait/Pas de Calais, the busiest shipping lane in the world and getting busier. Swimmers share the water with ships like the *Seawise Giant* at 458 metres long, 69 metres wide, with a draught of 25 metres and 350 metres high. When fully laden with 4.1 million barrels of crude oil, it weighs 648,000 tonnes. There is a very limited view from the bridge, but even if other objects are spotted, they cannot stop or even change course in time to avert a disaster. One fifth of all the vessels passing through are carrying dangerous goods and the Strait is where they all converge. The twenty miles of sea separating England and France is not the furthest recognized endurance swim in the world, but the tidal stream, the unpredictable weather and the shipping make it the toughest challenge. In both 2012 and 2013, swimmers died making solo attempts. More people have climbed Everest than have successfully swum the Channel. The French don't allow swimmers to attempt to cross from their coastline. Even though it would be an easier crossing than starting from England, due to the tides, they consider the crossing to be too dangerous. The Channel Swimming Association's handbook sums up the challenge:

It is quite possible to be ten miles from shore on a pitch-black, cold night, with a cresting sea, a three-knot tidal stream, and thirty metres of depth underneath... In such conditions, the Channel is no place for a physical weakling.

I booked my crossing with one of the recognized pilots. Each morning I woke before six and as I swam each day, I slowly felt my old speed returning. Speed was one thing, but how would I know if I could last in a cold sea for hour after hour? There was only one way to find out and that was to move my training from the pool to the sea, but I knew that would have to wait until later that year, when the sea temperature was bearable. In the meantime, I contacted my old swimming club and arranged to train with the Masters (a polite term for "old gits"!).

Twenty-six years after my last training session with my old swimming club, I found myself getting changed in the same changing room. To my complete surprise, I recognized several of the same swimmers I had trained and competed with all those years ago. But an even greater shock was in store. On the poolside was my old coach, Ted. He gave me a hug and I felt as if I was home. He hadn't changed; he still used the same jokes and rude expressions. I knew he would get me across the Channel, if anyone could.

"Where's Mick?" I asked. Ted and Mick had been inseparable as coaches.

"He died two years ago. This club was his life and when he stopped coaching, he fell ill. We had a good memorial service – 300 people turned up." For a moment neither of us said anything; we just shared a sense of loss.

"Come on then, Lord Larcombe; let's see what you can do. We'll try you in the fast lane."

The next hour was very painful.

CHAPTER 34

Step 5

**We admitted to God, to ourselves,
and to another human being the
exact nature of our wrongs**

Over the years, the number of people I kept in touch with from
school, university or the Army had dwindled. Now, whenever I met
someone for the first time, or bumped into someone from my past,
I didn't hide the truth and made sure I was brutally honest about
my life. Most people were a bit wary of this person who had so
recently self-destructed. One exception was Steve.

I began to attend the same church my mother attended. With
a congregation of several hundred, there were a lot of people
my own age there. I liked Steve the very first time I met him. He
struck me as an honest, kind and no-nonsense type of person. The
antithesis of the stereotypical church-going male, he had a highly
successful recycling business and his handshake was as strong as
any car-crusher. He'd overcome an addiction that had almost stolen
his life, and lived with the knowledge that he had probably provided
the drugs that had killed a close friend. Like me, he was married to
a northern lass and his children were the same age as mine. I don't
know anyone more genuine, honest and generous than Steve.

He had experienced things I couldn't even imagine. He'd been
jailed in India for selling drugs. When Steve was a teenager, his best

friend had bled to death on top of him as they both lay trapped following a high-speed car crash. He'd also lost his younger brother in an accident. Despite these setbacks, Steve was open and friendly and had a real heart for anyone suffering from addiction. I found I could talk to him about the last few years and he never once judged me. He just encouraged me and offered advice if and when I asked for it.

I still had a big step to take. I needed to admit to myself that my behaviour had been wrong. I had to take responsibility for all the damage I had caused. It has been a real help to me to tell Steve about all the things I had done. Confessing and admitting all the wrong is an important part of recovery. Holding on to things and refusing to accept responsibility is a sure way to arrest recovery, and often leads to a recurrence of destructive behaviour. I was beginning to understand about recovery, but I still couldn't understand what had caused me to self-destruct. I needed to know why I had imploded in the space of three years, when I had so many good things in my life.

CHAPTER 35

Step 6

**We were entirely ready to have God
remove all these defects of character**

Although I had little money, I did have time. For the first time in my
adult life, I didn't have a job to go to. As well as swimming, I walked
for at least an hour each day. Walking through woods and across
the fields gave me time to think, to take stock and understand my
priorities. Gambling had crushed the creativity in me and now I felt
my imagination returning. As I walked I made up stories I could tell
my three boys.

Story-telling is in my blood. I grew up on my grandmother's
stories. Having published thirty-five books, she knew how to
record adventures. Mum has been published almost forty times.
Harry loved to listen to my silly stories which involved shark attacks
and heroic battles, but most of all he loved me to tell him ghost
stories. When he moved to Jersey, we made up a complex ghost
story based on the island, and each time I visited him I invented
another chapter. Jersey is an island steeped in folklore, superstition
and ghost stories, so we visited the sites of our fictional adventure
to make the story come alive. I began to write down the story as it
unfolded, but these early chapters were neglected as my gambling
habit took hold of me. I had saved those first few chapters on my
laptop, which was taken away on the day I lost my job.

Every morning I enjoyed talking with Mum over a cup of tea. It was a highlight of my day and we discussed a whole range of subjects. Mum loves to build people up and encourage them to try things outside their comfort zone. One morning, she asked me why I didn't write a book. I could give her no real answer and told her about the start I'd made before gambling took a hold. She asked me if I thought I could find the lost chapters. That morning, as soon as the telephone lines of my old company opened for business, I called them. To my surprise, they took the trouble to look for my document. They found it on the data base and sent it to me.

I discovered that I really enjoyed writing. I'd never had the time or patience to sit and write, but now I found it gave me a huge sense of peace and satisfaction. My creative side, that had been so repressed, began to blossom. I finished the novel, a ghost story with a historical context, in two months. I loved researching and developing the characters as I walked through the wintery countryside.

I began to notice the first signs of spring; I almost felt the earth stirring itself as though from a long slumber. As the days passed and the nightmare of my gambling receded, it felt as if I too was emerging from an extended winter hibernation. Walking gave me time to think, both clearly and honestly. I realized for the first time that I had become very selfish. Although I had already appreciated how hard it must have been for Emma to put up with me, for the first time I really felt it. I was ready to change; I already felt a change in my outlook on life. I also recognized that I had probably left it too late to save my marriage, that the damage had been too much. Trust is so hard to attain, but really easy to lose. I came to accept that I might never win back Emma's trust.

CHAPTER 36

Step 7

**We humbly asked God to remove
all our shortcomings**

I continued to attend the Monday night meetings at Gamblers Anonymous. The organization is very careful to respect the privacy of its membership and is fiercely independent. It's important for me to respect and acknowledge the privacy of what I have experienced behind closed doors. But I can say that the fellowship and support I found through GA, and in particular the wonderful friends I made, have played a huge part in my recovery. I have heard stories that have made me cry, made me laugh and made me want to run as fast as I can from any form of gambling.

Slowly, I found my reasons for attending were changing. I felt a transition from the need to go and get help, to a desire to go and give help. One evening the secretary of the group announced that he was taking a job overseas. We needed a new secretary. The role was primarily to meet new members and make sure they felt welcomed. I was very touched when the group voted for me. It's a job I love and take very seriously.

While I seemed to be taking tentative steps forward in my life, Emma was finding life harder and harder. She'd been incredibly strong to set up home on her own with the children. Her father and mother were a great support, but bringing up a child with additional physical and mental needs as well as a full-on, active three-year-old, with only erratic payments from me and state benefits to support her, was exhausting. Matthew's day always starts before six. Without a husband to share morning duties, the strain began to take its toll on Emma. I tried to travel as often as I could and once I made the eight-hour round trip in a day, so she could have a break, but it was expensive and not really sustainable.

The car made it possible for me to drive up there at least every other weekend to see the boys, and I always took Emma to buy food to keep them stocked up. This was always very difficult with Matthew in tow. One foggy Saturday afternoon, we braced ourselves and took Matthew and Oscar with us to the supermarket. Matthew was almost impossible to control in supermarkets; the noise and visual stimulants overloaded his senses, causing him to shout out or run madly in different directions. I made sure he was strapped into my trolley. With Oscar in Emma's trolley, we set off down the first aisle with our shopping list.

Loading the shopping bags into the car, I looked down and was surprised to see a pack of own-brand avocado pears in the pocket of my coat. They weren't on our list and I certainly hadn't picked them up. I was suddenly horrified as I realized I hadn't paid for them.

"Emma, I need to go back and pay for these. Matty must have put them in my pocket. I won't be long." I ran back into the store. I could have just put them back on a shelf, but for some reason I wanted to pay for them. When I came back outside, Emma was looking at me very strangely. I think she realized I had changed. That evening she said she wanted to make a go of our marriage.

I have so much respect for Emma for making that decision. It was contrary to everything her parents and friends were telling her. I cried when she told me. It was so unexpected. She said I looked happier and healthier, as well as being more caring and attentive. Considering that for the last three years I'd spent the best part of my waking hours fretting over one bet or another, it wasn't hard to be a better father.

Understandably, Emma was the only person who could see the change. No one else from our shared past wanted to see me or even talk to me. They wanted me out of Emma's life. Reconciliation with me meant Emma had chosen a path that would bring her into direct conflict with her parents and all her friends. She knew her parents would be angry and hurt if they found out we were back together. She just couldn't bring herself to tell them.

Although I understood why everyone counselled Emma against reconciliation, and I knew she had chosen a difficult path, I just wanted to dance. I felt I'd been given an unexpected and probably underserved second chance. To face the fact that I would never really be a father again had been hard to bear. Despite thick fog, as I drove back to Kent the following day my world was now a better, brighter place. The garden was growing and the birds were singing again.

CHAPTER 37

Step 8

We made a list of all persons we had harmed and became willing to make amends to them all

Just as I was coming to the end of the novel, I was offered a contract to join a project that would call on my experience in the insurance industry. It was well paid and allowed me to work from home, so I could keep up my writing. At the same time, my old company honoured a financial agreement relating to the shares I had once owned. Emma searched online for a possible new home for us all and, realizing I had burnt all my bridges in Derbyshire, she found a lovely cottage in a village close to my mother's house. It was big enough for the boys to have their own bedrooms and a garden to run about in. It even had enough space for a vegetable patch. I paid rent in advance and a date was fixed for me to move in. Emma and the boys would follow a few weeks later after the summer term was over. I visited a whole range of schools and Matthew was offered a place in the school we thought would most suit his complex requirements. We had little furniture, but with help from Mum, I found all we needed at a YMCA furniture warehouse.

With Emma's help, I made a list of all the people I had borrowed from over the years, or lied to or hurt in some way. I wrote letters to everyone. Some were very hard; others I found easy. On the whole, it was a very healing experience as I wrote cheques and apologized for what I had done. If I had been expecting letters of thanks and forgiveness in return, I would have been very disappointed. I hadn't expected to be welcomed back with open arms, but I was a bit surprised that I only had one reply.

I felt cross that people I had once been so close to still saw me as someone not to be trusted. I knew I had changed beyond all recognition, but for some reason I was surprised when others didn't even give me a chance to show them. My dad phoned occasionally and each time he asked the same thing with some trepidation, as though he expected me to be gambling again. Looking back, I completely understand why, but at the time I felt hurt. This ball of resentment that my recovery was being ignored seemed to grow inside me until it exploded one day with catastrophic results.

I knew Emma still loved me and she could see the boys needed me. She also knew how difficult it would be to bring the boys up on her own. But something had stopped her from telling her parents about her decision to move south and get back together with me. They still saw me as the person who had caused devastation in the life of their daughter. I should have understood this, I should have been patient, but as usual I dived in and signed a three-year lease on the property. When Emma told me she needed more time, rather than agreeing and being supportive I felt hurt. I felt my love for her was not being returned. The hurt turned to anger.

In late April, I received the keys to the house that was going to be our new home, a fresh start for us both. Although Emma had found the property and set up my viewing, she'd never actually visited it. I worked through the night to move the YMCA furniture into the rooms, put up curtains and fill the drawers with the few possessions I had. I wanted Emma to fall in love with the house when she visited it for the first time. Mum had given me some of her cutlery and plates. I had just finished putting everything away when Emma arrived with the boys.

It should have been a beautiful weekend. The bluebells were out in all their glory in the surrounding woodland; after a freezing winter, the sun was warm and the hedgerows were bursting into life. Emma loved the house, but rather than being pleased, she felt cross that I would be spending weeks on my own in this beautiful home while she continued to struggle alone with the boys in their tiny house. We couldn't take Matty out of school because he had special educational provision that would have been too complex to transfer mid-term. She hated the furniture and the fact that everything was in the wrong place. Our love, still so delicate and fragile, faltered and became crushed as we argued about trivial things. We didn't dare speak about the fundamental issues of my impatience and her fear of committing herself to me against the advice of friends and family.

The day after they left, Emma called me and bluntly told me she couldn't move down. Ever. She was seeing her solicitor and this time she was divorcing me. Her bluntness wasn't because she was being cruel. I think it took a lot of courage to say what she said, and she just felt she had to say it quickly while she could. She knew it would be devastating for me.

It was. I felt lost and alone. Yet again, I felt the abandonment that seemed to follow me. My emptiness and loss felt even worse than before. I knew it had been my fault the first time, and I could accept then that we were apart because of my behaviour. Now I wished we had never even tried to work it out because losing my family again, after I thought they were coming back, was a roller-coaster ride I could hardly endure.

I was alone in the house; my computer didn't have any gambling protection. I could have gambled and allowed myself to fall back into the pit. But it was a pit I knew I would never climb out of.

Instead I called Steve and talked it through.

"You need to let go," he said. "If it's meant to be, then she'll come back. I get the feeling patience is not one of your strengths. I think this will be good for you in the long term. You might not see it now because you're hurting, but you'll look back on this as a more patient person."

Wise words and also very true. Once, my pride would have stopped me from even *asking* for advice, let alone taking it on board, but now I listened intently. I needed to be more patient. The need to have everything right away was one of the flaws in my character that had kept me gambling. I was learning that, although some people are blessed with more patience than others, like a muscle patience can be developed.

I went for a swim, and that evening I drove to Gamblers Anonymous. My friends gathered round. Never once did I even consider placing a bet.

CHAPTER 38

Step 9

**We made direct amends to such people
whenever possible, except when to do
so would injure them or others**

It had been an unusually cold spring. Heavy snow had fallen much later than usual. As a result the sea temperature was much lower than normal for early May. As I stood on the shingle looking out across the Dover Strait towards France, the slate-grey horizon was almost indistinguishable from the sky. I wanted to see France, but all I could see was mile after daunting mile of intimidating water.

"What's your name, love?" Freda asked, as I tried not to shiver against the chilling on-sea breeze that felt more like a gale. I told her my name and she gave me a card with a number on it. Freda is a legend to all Channel swimmers. Every Saturday and Sunday between May and October, she sits by the breakwater at Dover harbour, for hour after hour, providing a safe environment for hopeful Channel soloists and relay swimmers. No one can remember a time before Freda. No one knows how old she is.

"When's your swim?" she asked.

"Next August," I said, feeling I was letting her down by not having a go that very day.

"OK," she said. "Give me an hour and then see how you feel. Make sure you team up with someone else and don't go far out. If you can't see me, I can't flippin' well see you." An efficient-looking lady gave me a yellow swim cap and wrote my number on a clipboard and then on my hand with a big, black felt-tip pen.

By now about twenty other swimmers had checked in and stripped down to their trunks or costumes, and were all chatting together. My teeth were the only part of me that felt like chatting and I left it until the very last minute to strip off. A friendly grey-haired man called me over and rubbed my arms and neck with a fatty substance. Contrary to popular belief, Channel swimmers are unlikely to smother themselves in goose fat to keep warm. Instead, a Vaseline-based mixture stops the skin chaffing in the salty water and provides some protection against jellyfish stings. It certainly doesn't provide any warmth.

"How long are you doing today?" he asked me. I was doing all I could not to shiver as the cold wind blew in off the sea.

"I'm going to do an hour and then see how I go. My attempt isn't until next year." Again, I felt myself apologizing.

"Good for you. That's it, take it nice and slow." I didn't think one hour in the freezing water was taking it nice and slow, but I followed the crowd down to the waterfront and then tried to hide my gasp from the other swimmers as the freezing water swallowed me. After about six strokes my head went numb. After twelve, my head ached and other parts of my body went numb. Soon I felt completely numb and my whole body ached. I tried to keep pace with another swimmer, but after a few minutes he was lost in the waves. Or was I the one lost? Every time I turned my head to the left I was hit by a wave and I swallowed a mouthful of salty water that made me gag. I felt my tongue swelling from all the salt. After what seemed like an age I stopped to tread water. I checked my waterproof watch. I'd only been in the water for ten minutes. I was disheartened. Already I was worried about my feet. Everything below the ankle was completely numb. At one stage I reached down in the murky water to check if my feet were actually still attached to my legs.

Somehow I managed to stay out in the freezing water for fifty minutes. My whole body was shivering. I swam back towards the beach, which was now filled by about fifty swimmers in red caps. These were the relay swimmers (a much more civilized but less challenging way of crossing the Channel), getting into the water as I was getting out. Or at least trying to get out. I couldn't feel my legs. The waves crashed over me as I tried to find my feet and stand up on the steep shingle at the water's edge. I tried and tried, but I just could not stand up. To all the swimmers just getting in, I must have looked like a beached whale, rolling about in the surf. No one offered to help me. Somehow I managed to pull myself clear of the waves, but I still had to find my feet and walk up to the top of the beach.

It was as I crawled/dragged myself up the beach that I realized the enormity of the challenge I had set myself. But there was worse to come. I couldn't get myself dressed. My fingers were numb and my tired limbs just weren't functioning. Eventually I managed to get my clothes back on. I mumbled something to Freda about coming back again next week, but my lips wouldn't work; my whole face was immobilized by the cold. I think what I actually said was, "Blanksbleeder, bleeblack mextmeek." She gave me a strange look as I hobbled off, shaking violently and blue with cold.

I found a café and tried to drink a hot chocolate, but, unable to hold the cup, I spilled most of the scalding liquid in my lap. I sat in the car with the heating on full. The sun burnt away the haze, but I kept my heater on for the whole hour's drive back. I didn't stop shivering until I was home. I contemplated giving up on the idea of swimming the Channel, but only very briefly. On Monday, I was back in the pool. I swam for three hours and then had a sauna.

The following week I managed two hours in the sea. I also managed to get out of the water. I felt proud of myself until Freda put me in my place.

"What are you doing getting out? The way you walked up the beach tells me you still have some energy left." I was still numb, and could hardly drive home, I was shaking so much. The next week I was prepared to do longer, but it was blowing a gale and Freda pulled us all out after an hour. We all huddled round her, draped in our towels, and she said it was only the second time in all her years of coaching that she had had to do that. No one knew how many years that was, but we all knew it was a very long time. I felt quite encouraged when a swimmer next to me threw up from sea-sickness. Each week Freda made me do an extra hour. Soon, my body became more used to the cold, and the sea gradually warmed.

I kept a diary of each swim. Here's an entry from Saturday, 6 August 2013:

Six hours!!!! Clear day, but very choppy. Tough conditions – now qualified for Channel swim. Might have done longer, but arms felt painful and back hurt from two-hour point. Only a few swimmers left at the end!! I can do this!!!

PS: Remembered to hobble slowly up beach today in case Freda sent me back in!

The six-hour swim is a magic number. It's the qualification swim for a Channel crossing. I needed to be doing six hours on Saturday and Sunday every week, plus the pool work. Long swims are complicated by feeding, which involves swimming back to the shore after two hours for a "feed" (a warm carbohydrate drink and a jelly baby!), and then regular feeds on the hour after that for up to eight hours. My biggest problem was boredom. As I swam up and down between the harbour walls, I couldn't help thinking of all the fun things a normal person would be doing on a Saturday.

One Monday evening in mid July I saw the tragic news that one of Freda's swimmers, Susan Taylor, had died just a mile off the French coast. It came as a huge shock. Susan had been looking forward to her attempt and had trained really hard. The endurance community is quite close-knit and the following Saturday we had a minute's silence in her memory. Freda cried as she said a few words and then we got straight back in the water. Susan was the eighth person to die attempting to cross the Channel and the second in two years. She was thirty-four.

CHAPTER 39

Step 10

**We continued to take personal inventory and
when we were wrong, promptly admitted it**

It was a lovely sunny summer's day. The kind of day when you
wonder why you'd ever want to holiday abroad. Temperatures were
soaring and I was looking forward to lunch at my local, The Chaser
Inn, with Andrew Meade, my mum's and now my own financial
adviser.

We found an outside table. As we both tucked into our cheese
ploughman's lunches, Andrew said, "I've just seen something I am
struggling to understand."

I was intrigued. I didn't think there could be much Andrew
didn't understand.

He went on, "I just came from a newsagents and there was a
young lady in the queue ahead of me. I think she had just got her
benefit cheque from the post office counter. When it was her turn
at the till, she asked for twenty Benson and Hedges and 200 scratch
cards! Did I mishear her?"

"Probably not. Poor thing, she's probably spent the last few
days imagining what she'll do with the money if she wins. All the
debt she'll repay, the houses and cars she'll buy, how she'll treat her
friends and stick her fingers up to her boss. The reality is, though,
that she's going to go hungry this week."

"How are things with Emma?" he asked, wiping beer froth from his beard.

"I've come to terms with the fact that I've lost them. I am going up as often as I can and they still come down occasionally. Emma's really good about access and she makes a real effort to travel. I told Harry we'd split up. I was really worried about how he might take that. He loves Emma to bits, calls her Dandelion. He doesn't know why we split, but I'll have to tell him one day." It felt quite good to share my feelings with Andrew. He'd been so helpful to me and now I counted him as a friend.

"Are you still hopeful of reconciliation?"

"I still love Emma and I miss the boys so much, especially at night. I often imagine them choosing their favourite books, and I wish I could read to them till they fall asleep, like I used to. I still cry myself to sleep a few times a week. The truth is, I'm still hopeful, but I'm also realistic. I had my chance. It's time to let her go and move on. I just try to be the best father I can be."

In spite of my words, I didn't realize how tightly I was still holding on to a last strand of hope. When I got home there was a letter waiting for me on the doormat. It was from Emma's solicitors. It stated that she was seeking a divorce on the grounds of my unreasonable behaviour. Then it listed everything horrible I had ever done. The sad thing was, it was all true. The letter I was holding had become soaking wet from my tears, I guess I'd been hoping more than I realised. I wasn't expecting the letter. It hit me like a broadside from a battle cruiser. I sat down at the kitchen table, put my head in my hands and wailed. I hope the neighbours weren't in their garden sunbathing.

Chapter 40

Step 11

**We sought through prayer and meditation
to improve our conscious contact with God,
praying only for knowledge of His will for
us and power to carry that out**

The *Daily Mail* changed my life dramatically overnight. Several
weeks before the double-page feature was published, a friend who
worked in local radio had casually mentioned my story to her boss.
He interviewed me and the piece went on air later that week. I
wanted people to know there was a downside to gambling; that,
although most people gambled responsibly, there were some whose
lives were destroyed. There is so much advertising and glamour
surrounding the industry, I just wanted people to know the darker,
dirtier side. Until now very few people have been willing to come
out and talk about their experiences. There is a stigma attached
to gambling addiction. Alcoholism and drug addiction seem to be
almost acceptable, or at least understood. Gambling addicts are not
understood at all. I have heard people ask, "Why didn't you just
stop?" Now I wanted to warn people of the dangers.

For the majority of my life, I had tried to live up to the
expectations of others. In the Army, a Sword of Honour winner is
expected to become a General; in swimming my coaches expected
me to get to the very top. The constant pressure to succeed and

be seen as successful had caused me stress and had financially stretched me. I always wanted people to think the best of me, and sometimes that meant I became the person I thought they expected me to be and not the person I truly was.

Now I wanted to be myself, warts and all. I found it incredibly refreshing to be honest, and I made a promise to myself that I would hold true to my personal integrity and try my best not to compromise my core beliefs and my faith in Christ. Although I can remember feeling quite nervous before the radio interview was broadcast, I was prepared to take all the criticism I thought would come my way. After all, I'd caused so much pain and I was the only one to blame.

People were genuinely shocked by my story, but I didn't ever receive any criticism. Instead people commented on how brave I was for speaking out. My interview generated a lot of debate, and soon I was invited to the BBC for a live radio interview, and a BBC TV crew came to film me at home for an interview on local TV. I learned very quickly that the length of time spent filming bears no correlation to the edited end product.

On the other hand, a two-page feature for the local paper with photographs does mean the topic can be explored in greater depth. A feature by the *Kent and Sussex Courier* the following week was well-balanced and hard-hitting. There was absolutely no chance for me to feel any sense of self-importance. I knew people were only interested in my story because it was so shocking and unpleasant. I did feel a bit like the freak at a circus show. I can remember feeling relieved that the story was only a local one and that my old work colleagues and all Emma's friends and family wouldn't have seen it. And then I had a call from a *Daily Mail* reporter.

I didn't have to speak to them. I wasn't offered any money. I wasn't selling my story for cash; I just felt that the story had to be told. I wanted people to know what a problem gambling was for some; that there were people suffering because of it; and that anyone could become addicted. If I could be brave enough to go through with this media exposure, I might be able to help someone to keep a family together. However, I also wanted to protect Emma and the boys from anything that might cause them upset. If I was going to go through with this, I would have to tell Harry everything; I couldn't run the risk of him just reading it, or being teased at school. I thought about it, took advice from friends and prayed about it. And then I agreed to talk.

One Saturday morning in mid August we were travelling down to Devon, to the same village by the sea where I had enjoyed my childhood holidays. There was no way we could all fit into my old Honda, so I hired a large estate car for Emma, the boys and me. In the end Emma didn't want to travel with me and took her own car. We would all be together in the same apartment for a week, but her car gave her freedom to escape if it all got too much. I didn't argue, but I was secretly disappointed not to be sitting with her for five hours.

It was hot on the motorway and the boys needed to stop. I called Emma and told her I was pulling over at the next service station. It was only when I walked past the newspapers in WHSmith that I remembered. Today was the day. I bought the paper while Emma looked after the boys. It was almost completely accurate and designed for maximum impact. More than 5 million people read the paper that weekend. Emma was one of them. She'd been called by her family and bought her own copy; a crisis was brewing. They were not happy. Neither was Harry's mother, who had been told about the article by friends and was now convinced I'd made thousands by spilling the beans.

Telling Harry, now twelve years old, was one of the hardest things I have ever done as a parent. We have always been close. One of our mantras is "Harry doesn't lie to Daddy and Daddy doesn't lie to Harry". This time I had to tell Harry I had lied through my teeth for three years, at the cost of my marriage, my job and all my money.

It takes five hours to walk the seven miles from Thurlstone to Salcombe along the undulating coastal path. It was the same route I had followed with my mother when, as a child, she told me about my ancestors. The cliffs rise hundreds of feet above the sea in places. It wasn't the first time Harry and I had walked this path between two of the most glorious places in South Devon. The first time Harry had begged me to tell him ghost stories and when I ran out, he asked for a history of the Second World War. This time, I had no idea where to begin the conversation. I felt as though I had let him down. In the end, I showed him the article before we set off, and the rest came naturally.

When I had finished, Harry looked at me with his brown eyes. Gulls shrieked as they circled above us, taking advantage of the warm air currents driven up by the steep rock formations. The sea was shimmering below us like a crystal blanket. He smiled and simply said: "Daddy, you really messed up. Just make sure you don't do it again."

Those words meant so much to me. I thought I would lose his love, his trust and his respect, but he didn't criticize me or, worse, storm off in a silent strop. He just accepted it was something that had happened, and now I had a chance to put things right.

Later in the holiday I took Harry mackerel fishing. I wondered if he would remember the day as I remembered my own fishing trip with Dad to Lyme Regis almost forty years ago. I hope he does. My phone rang as we were passing The Bar, a lethal hidden rock in the mouth of the Salcombe Estuary.

"Hi, my name is Karen. I'm calling from ITV's *Lorraine* programme. We saw your story in the *Daily Mail*. Can I talk to you?"

The following week I took Harry with me to the ITV studio in south London. He loved the experience. One of his favourite pop stars was being interviewed just before me and I took a photo of the two of them as we left the studio. The star was mobbed by a crowd of fans and photographers, while I found a taxi and felt completely vulnerable, washed out and exposed. I had agreed to let them show some pictures of my happy life, before I had destroyed it. In the taxi my mobile bleeped, buzzed, flashed, vibrated and even made noises I had never heard before. There were texts, emails and missed-call alerts. I had suggested, live on TV, that if anyone thought they had a problem with gambling, or knew someone who did, they should send me a tweet.

I spent the next week answering messages from the friends and families of people who were betting compulsively, or from gamblers who felt they were not in control of their lives. Even more messages came flooding in after I gave a half-hour interview on Radio 5 Live. Harry could see that I was helping other people and didn't mind when I took a call in the middle of a game we were playing. He went home that summer and explained to his mum how I was able to reach people who were really suffering. When she saw Harry was standing by me, she accepted my motives and has since been very supportive. Emma, on the other hand, was still angry with me for going public. That is, until her tennis coach changed everything.

Like me, Emma gets tired and stressed with life unless she exercises regularly. Tennis had long been a way for her to vent her frustration. She had known Dave, her tennis coach, for many years before she met me. They have a mutual respect and understanding for each other. Emma had no idea Dave was a gambler. In fact, I don't think Emma knew anyone who gambled other than me. It was early September and the boys had just begun their new term at school and nursery. Emma called Dave and arranged an hour of tennis. Before they played, Emma sensed he wanted to talk about something.

Dave was a regular gambler. He thought he was in control, but his fiancée did not. She refused to marry him until he stopped gambling. They had been engaged for a long time. One Sunday morning in August, they were reading the papers together and she passed him the paper.

"Look at this – it seems quite relevant. You probably know this guy. He lived up here," she said.

Dave didn't know me, but he instantly recognized that the Emma in the article was someone he knew well. He told Emma that, as he read the article, he had a strange feeling – something really significant. He felt the words having a profound effect on him. He recognized that his gambling behaviour patterns were similar to mine. He clearly saw that he had a problem and decided there and then to stop gambling. "Your husband saved my marriage – a marriage that was never going to even happen until I admitted I had a problem. I haven't had a single bet since I read it six weeks ago; and this week, we fixed a date for the wedding. Please can you thank Justyn for me?"

Dave's words, in turn, had a profound effect on Emma. This was a man she respected and trusted, and he too had a problem with gambling. He also had a strong faith. Tears rolling down his cheeks, he told Emma that he felt very strongly that despite all the hurt I had caused, God wanted us to get back together. Emma laughed and told him that would never happen, that we were getting a divorce. But, from that day on, Emma's attitude to me changed significantly. She quite suddenly and dramatically understood why I felt it was so important to share my story. She didn't question my motives and we began to chat about normal things, to agree and even laugh occasionally.

One month later I received a tweet from someone who had been following my story – a guy of about my age, who came from wealthy Indian family. Over the course of the previous five years he had gambled away all his money. He was lost and alone, not able to tell his wife. When he saw the article, completely by chance on an aeroplane one day, he recognized elements of himself and realized he wasn't alone. We linked up, and just talking about the issue with someone who understands has been a great help to him.

I suffered as a result of going public. My old company, quite correctly, sent me a letter from their solicitor reminding me of my confidentiality clause. My consulting work, my only source of income, was also at stake when I was found guilty of bringing my industry into disrepute. However, both organizations recognized that I wasn't trying to sensationalize my life; I just wanted to reach out and help others.

I found an immense sense of liberty in being so open about my private life. I had always strived to be the best, it mattered to me how people saw me or thought of me. Now, they knew my faults; I had no expectation to live up to. That set me free to be myself. I had nothing left to hide.

More and more people were coming forward and opening up. The most important advice I could ever give was not to hide the habit, but to share and get help before it was too late.

Although I felt good knowing I could help others, every time I thought about Emma I felt my own loss. Until the day I finally decided to really let go.

CHAPTER 41

Step 12

Having had a spiritual awakening as the result of these steps, we try to carry this message to others and to practise these principles in all our affairs

The letter had been on my desk for three days. I knew exactly what was inside the neatly sealed envelope. I recognized the name of the family law firm, the Nottingham address. I wanted to be able to call Emma "my wife" for just a few more days. I wanted to open the letter when I was feeling strong, and now that time had come. I couldn't put it off any longer.

It was a very formal letter from the divorce court. Unless I had any final objections, I was requested to sign the papers and return them to the court. I cried as I signed my name. I cried for Matthew and Oscar, who would become officially fatherless, except every other weekend. I cried for Emma and the pain I had caused her, the dreams I had stolen along with her beautiful smile. And I cried for myself, for the loss of my best friend and the huge gap she would leave in my life. It's about a mile from my house to the nearest postbox. The last light of day faded from the late-October sky as I set off along the lane. It was almost exactly a year since I had left our family home for the last time, and now the falling leaves reminded me of my final walk with Emma to the duck pond.

I remembered the times we had walked together hand in hand, laughing at something, nothing and everything.

I had tried so hard over the previous year to fix everything, to make it right, but some things, I realized, just couldn't be mended. There were consequences that went with my behaviour. When I saw the postbox ahead, I slowed my pace. I wanted just a few more minutes. I leaned against the postbox, until I realized I could find no more reasons to delay the inevitable, but it still took both my hands to force the letter through the slot. And then I let go. The letter dropped. I pictured myself handing Emma back to my Creator at the cross, and I felt stronger for it.

The journey back home seemed twice the distance. I sent Emma a text as I walked. I told her I had signed and sent the letter, that I would always love her, and that I wished her a happy life and hoped she would find someone better than me, who would treat her properly; someone with whom she could share her dreams. I said I was sorry. Then I said goodbye.

That Sunday I was invited to share my story at a church in Tunbridge Wells. I really didn't think anyone from the congregation would want to hear a story about a recovering addict. But I was surprised. I spoke for forty-five minutes and I could see people were really listening. At the end, people came up to me and shared their concerns about friends or relatives who they thought might be struggling with gambling. I also spoke to a man who told me he had suffered from an addiction for several years before he attended the Recovery Course, a Christ-centred programme based on the twelve steps. I took the details because I was beginning to feel I wanted to help others in a more deliberate way and share more openly about how my faith had been such a help to my recovery; something I couldn't really do at Gamblers Anonymous, where a "god of your own understanding" is all you can really discuss!

I really enjoyed talking at that church and was greatly encouraged when I received a lovely letter from a lady who had listened to me speak. The final words of her letter really summed up my journey:

"Every blessing to you, someone with a passion for the broken-hearted, that you will find the depth of healing you need, from the only One who can give it."

Later that day I shared a cup of tea with Mum. She told me that the church where I had just spoken was the very first church she had spoken at just after she had been healed. I have seen a great many "coincidences" in my life since I stopped gambling and put my faith back in my Creator.

It is important that, as a recovering addict, I only take one day at a time. I love that. It sets me free to enjoy today, not to worry about what tomorrow might bring, or where I need to be in one year, two years or five years in terms of my career path, my promotions, my salary grade. I feel so liberated to be able to be myself. But at what cost? I can't look back – that's the beauty of living in the now. One day at a time means letting go of yesterday as well as tomorrow.

The Prayer for Serenity means so much to me. It's a prayer adopted by many of the Anonymous fellowships that help so many people:

> *God, grant me the serenity to accept the things*
> *I cannot change,*
> *The courage to change the things I can,*
> *And wisdom to know the difference.*

REINHOLD NIEBUHR

CHAPTER 42

Reflection

Humility is an honest approach to the reality of our own lives and acknowledges that we are not more important than other people.

ABBOT CHRISTOPHER JAMISON

I don't have an answer as to what caused me to gamble so destructively. I am sure I have a gene or a predisposition to addictive behaviour. But it seems a little strange that it didn't manifest itself until I was forty. That would lead me to conclude that there were environmental circumstances that also contributed. I will let you, the reader, make up your own mind about some of the things that may have triggered my addiction. One thing I am convinced of is that addictions of all types usually cover over an underlying emotional issue.

Russell Brand, in an article he wrote in the *Spectator* magazine, makes the point that: "Drugs and alcohol are not my problem – reality is my problem. Drugs and alcohol are my solution. I look to drugs and booze to fill up a hole in me."

Unlike drug and alcohol addictions, gambling is progressive rather than chemical. It could be the repetitive nature of gambling and the progressive secretion of adrenaline in the brain when betting that cause addiction. Some people are immediately hooked after one bet. That didn't really happen to me. For me, my circumstances, the opportunity to gamble, the availability of money, my competitive nature, my all-or-nothing attitude, my optimism and my pride were all contributing factors.

I am no psychologist or professor of addictive behaviour. This is not a recovery manual. I just want to share my story in the hope that, in a world of instant gratification and a growing social acceptance of gambling as a legitimate activity, the truth that gambling can and does shatter lives will be accepted and acknowledged by the public, the betting industry and the government.

There has been a huge increase in gambling advertising since 2005. I sense people are becoming tired of it. People who have never gambled are sent invitations on their social media timelines. Popular programmes, enjoyed by the young, are sponsored by betting companies. But I believe the tide is now turning. I want to warn people about the dangers of gambling, to try and balance the constant bombardment of invitations to sign up for a free bet.

I recently addressed a committee of peers at the House of Lords. A debate was taking place about the impact of one-stop-shop self-exclusion, allowing problem gamblers to exclude themselves from the hundreds, if not thousands, of online betting sites in one go. I know that if I had done that when I first excluded myself from the one site I visited, it would have had a huge impact on my life. Perhaps my family would never have split up.

The week after I gave that first talk in public, Emma rang me. She was in tears and obviously distressed about something. I asked her what the matter was.

"It's you. I can't do it. I still... I still love you."

"Ah. Well, that might change things a bit," I said.

It did change things. We talked for an hour and this time I was patient. I listened more than I spoke and told her to take her time, that there was no rush, that we had a lifetime to get it right. There are no words to describe the happiness I felt, the overflowing joy, or the total and complete gratitude I had towards Emma for giving me another chance. When I had placed that first £5 bet, I had gone on to lose so much more than my money, my wife's money, my house and my job. I lost the trust of my wife, my closest friend. But now, Emma was trusting me again.

I have found recovery. I am now completely debt free, for the very first time since my dad gave me a loan as a teenager. I can't look back and think about the three quarters of a million pounds I squandered and where we might be if it had been invested properly. All I can do is look forward.

I have trained as a money advisor and I now give debt advice in my spare time with West Kent Debt Advice. They helped me when I needed them most. It's time to give something back. Roughly half of all their clients have underlying addictions, but it's often the debt problems that cause marriages to break down. I know what it feels like when there is not enough money to pay the bills, and the pressures that can put on a relationship. I know how hard it is to juggle payday-loan repayments and to dread a phone call. I understand what it feels like to receive red chasing letters and to lie awake at night worrying about debt. I want to help people find a way through, to let them know there are people who care. And a God who cares. It starts at home, and Emma and I will budget our finances monthly, weekly and even daily. I can't hide anything from her and I don't want to.

I don't cry myself to sleep at night. I read stories to my boys and lie next to them as their breathing slows and sleep washes over them. Then I go and talk to my wife – a woman I lost and now have no intention of losing again. I make sure I try to do more listening than talking, but I'm not perfect.

There is a small leather-bound book on my desk. It was one of the things I put in my bin liner on the day my pride was finally broken. From time to time I flick through the hand-written pages. It contains some very private notes I made between 2004 and 2009. The notes are brutally honest. They contain aspirations, New Year resolutions, my goals and my dreams. There's an entry dated 7 March 2004, the day I met Emma:

Reflection

Today I met my future wife. She doesn't know it yet. Think I have a lot of work to do!

Most entries seem to be about finances: how to manage them and reminders to myself to be careful. I only got halfway through the book. My last entry was in September 2009, the month I placed my first bet. It's no coincidence. Let me share what I wrote:

Matty needs so much care. A big challenge lies ahead. Must read my Bible more often and stay close to Emma. Not sure if we will cope otherwise.

One month ago, almost five years after the last note, I made another entry. I just copied the same words. This time I intend to pay heed.

I still don't really know how I fell from having it all to having less than nothing. I feel privileged that many of the important things are back: my family, my self-respect, my values. Maybe I am even better off than before, because now I know what is important: honesty, family, friendship, love. And I know that what glitters the most may not be the most important: wealth, career, popularity. I feel privileged that I found a path of recovery before I ended my life. This book is dedicated to those who have yet to find their own recovery and those who never did before it was too late. I have come to think that *why* it all happened in my life is not as important as *how* my life will be. Every day I don't gamble is a good day. I want the rest of my life to be good.

Epilogue

I am ready. I have an experienced pilot who knows the Channel well – its tides, its climate and character, the busy shipping that will cross my path. I trust him to do his job. I'll just get my head down, stay close to the boat and swim with every ounce of strength I have for the shores of France. I've trained hard for this and now it's time to put myself to the test. I have been told I will lose several kilograms in body weight during this challenge; that there will be times when I will dream of giving up, packing it all in, getting in the boat and taking the easy way out. Only time will tell if I am up to this challenge. And the prize? There is no gold medal, or winner's cheque; just a sense of pride and a feeling of satisfaction that I have fronted up to human frailty and the worst that nature can throw at me, and stood the test. I will have overcome.

But first there are some people who need my help.

It's 7 p.m. and the guests are still arriving. I wasn't expecting this many. I hope there's enough food to go round. This is no party; there are no cocktails served here – the guests are all addicts. Every Wednesday evening for the next fourteen weeks, these people will explore recovery using the Twelve-Step Recovery Programme and practical verses from the Bible, the best life guide I ever read. I'll share my experiences, but more importantly I'm praying that through group work and discussion, the guests will find recovery from their different addictions. They'll be surprised to find that they aren't the only ones with a problem and that, by talking about it, things start to get better. My hope is that their children will still have a dad and/or a mum to love them and look after them, that they can start to live life to the full and not be dragged down by a destructive pattern of behaviour that steals their money, their self-respect and their health.

Things are looking up; spring is on the way. There are signs that the laws relating to gambling are being amended to protect those most vulnerable. I am regularly asked to comment on gambling or debt in the media. The broadcasters like a political angle. But I am not anti-gambling. Three quarters of all adults in the UK gamble regularly, but just under 1 per cent of them are compulsive gamblers. The gaming industry says that's a tiny percentage, so let's not worry too much. But that tiny percentage is 500,000 people. People whose lives are devastated and broken. That's too many. One is too many.

Next time you walk down your High Street, take a look through the windows of those shops with bright colours – the ones offering free bets, free tea and coffee. Some of these shops have windows that don't let you see inside. Take a look at the glass anyway and when you see your reflection, be honest with yourself. Is there something in your life you need some help with? Or maybe you're worried about someone you love. Are they spending too much time chasing something that really has no value?

If not, be glad. "There but for the grace of God go I."

Contact the author

Since The Daily Mail Article on Saturday 17th August 2013, I have been contacted by many people with gambling addictions and also by friends and family of compulsive gamblers. There is currently little provision for those suffering form this crippling addiction. There is help available and hope for recovery. I want to encourage anyone who is suffering through a gambling problem either as addicts themselves or those effected by the actions of others close to them, to make contact.

They can do this directly using Twitter: **@justynlarcombe** is a site dedicated to recovery; or email me at **justyn.larcombe@ btinternet.com**

GamCare offers phone support on 0808 8020 133. They also offer counseling where required. They have an online self assessment if you are worried or unsure about your gambling activity. There is also free advice available online at www.gamcare.org.uk

Gamblers Anonymous is a fellowship of men and women who have joined together to do something about problem gambling and to help others do the same. There may be groups meeting in your area. They also have a connected group for victims of gambling. Details can be found at: www.gamblersanonymous.org.uk

Betknowmore UK (BKM) also offer an outreach mentoring service: "Betknowmore UK is a social enterprise, set up to develop and deliver education, support and mentoring services to address issues around problem gambling." Details can be found at: www. betknowmoreuk.org

Don't suffer in silence. There is help available.
Be honest with others and be honest with yourself.